Quilt Lab

The Creative Side of Science

12 Clever Projects

Alexandra Winston

stashBOOKS
an imprint of C&T Publishing

Text copyright © 2014 by Alexandra Winston

Photography and Artwork copyright © 2014 by C&T Publishing, Inc.

Publisher: Amy Marson

Creative Director: Gailen Runge

Art Director: Kristy Zacharias

Editor: S. Michele Fry

Technical Editors: Helen Frost and Debbie Rodgers

Cover/Book Designer: April Mostek

Production Coordinator: Jenny Davis

Production Editor: Joanna Burgarino

Illustrator: Kirstie Petterson

Photo Assistant: Mary Peyton Peppo

Photography by Diane Pedersen and Nissa Brehmer of C&T Publishing, Inc.,
unless otherwise noted

Library of Congress Cataloging-in-Publication Data

Winston, Alexandra, 1984-

 Quilt lab : the creative side of science : 12 clever projects / Alexandra Winston.

   pages cm

 ISBN 978-1-60705-803-8 (soft cover)

1. Patchwork--Patterns. 2. Quilting--Patterns. 3. Patchwork--Patterns--
Design. I. Title.

 TT835.W552 2014

 746.46--dc23

                          2013023072

Printed in China

10 9 8 7 6 5 4 3 2 1

Dedication

To Josh, whose opinions, support, and knowledge were invaluable to making this book (even if I seemed to ignore them all)

Acknowledgments

Big thanks to everyone who helped me along the way!

Mom, who taught me how to sew and who gave me my creativity and craftiness

Roxane Cerda, who dug through a stack of proposals and picked mine

Michele Fry, who answered tons of silly emails from me

My team: Joanna, Helen, Debbie, Jenny, Nissa, Diane, Kirstie, and everyone else at C&T who checked my work and brought this book to life

Kate McKean, agent extraordinaire

The ladies of QG, who keep me up to date on what's hot, inspire me constantly, and make sewing fun

My bloggy friends—Amanda, Darcy, Lindsey, and Melody—who encouraged me to keep going and shared their awesome advice and opinions

Free Spirit (freespiritfabric.com), who generously donated solids that were a pleasure to sew with

Contents

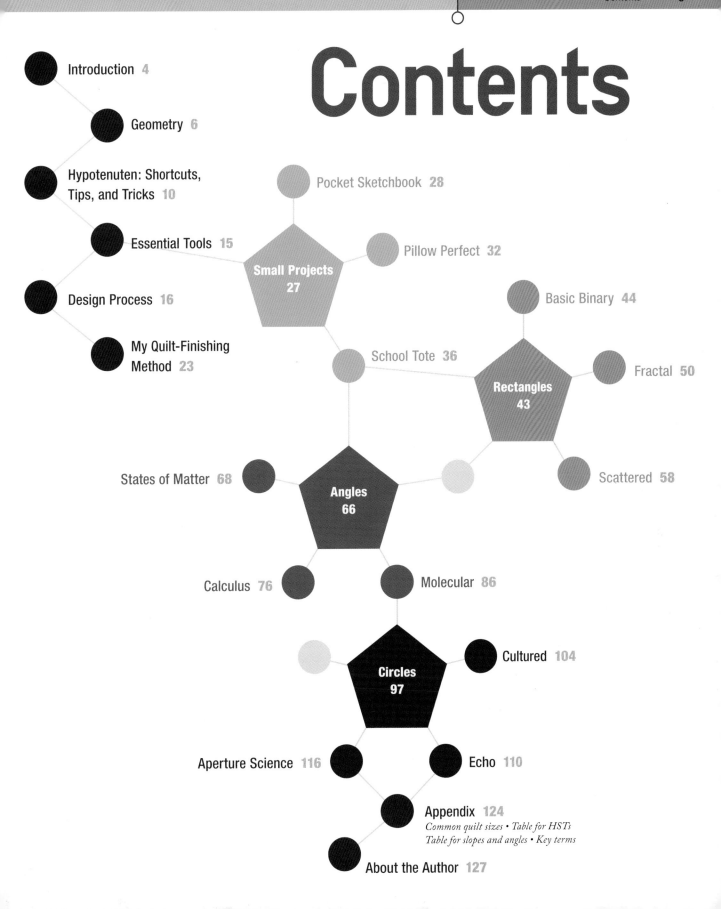

Introduction:
Where Science Meets Sewing

science |ˈsīəns| *noun—the intellectual and practical activity encompassing the systematic study of the structure and behavior of the physical and natural world through observation and experiment*

I love geeky things. I watch video games (yes, watch not play) and sci-fi shows. I adore math so much that I teach it. I even used the theme from *The Legend of Zelda* as the recessional song at my wedding. But *science* has never really been my best subject. In fact, my first C was in science class.

In high school I took a slight interest in chemistry, but only so far as to memorize what charge each element has—positive and negative numbers are a concept I'm more comfortable with. I always made someone else do the dissection in biology.

To me, science is overwhelming and complex, enormous and miniscule, concrete and nebulous. It encompasses a myriad of topics, from the body and nature to computers and synthetic materials. Science is about people and behaviors and planets and space and numbers and computers. I dare you to look up "fields of science" in Wikipedia and not be overwhelmed.

If you "read" science magazines as I do, then you have probably noticed the graphics. Oh, how I love looking at the pictures! My favorites used to be the pictures of the universe with all those colorful clouds—like looking at a dream. Then, not too long ago, my husband burst my bubble and told me that that's not how space really looks! Special cameras capture different light wavelengths, and then those (sneaky!) scientists assign colors.

That's when it occurred to me: Science is more than *understanding* all the theories and rules; science is about *communicating* these ideas with everyone who is interested. Science is about our surroundings and *us*. Those lovely pictures of space communicate what we can't see with the naked eye; they show us layers of information. A picture is worth a thousand words, and science is a deeply graphic discipline. What words cannot convey, images can. Images and graphs reduce the data to a form that everyone can appreciate and learn from.

I have taken many disciplines and ideas and turned them into quilts, trying to make the designs practical, educational, and attractive. I've drawn on basic ideas such as the states of matter and advanced concepts such as calculus; I even sneaked in my love of video games and photography. My quilt *Aperture Science* (page 116) is directly inspired by the game *Portal*. Each quilt has a story, a lesson, or an idea that underlies the design and fabrics and gives the quilt extra depth.

Disclaimer!

I'm a quilter–math teacher, not a scientist. With these designs I have taken some artistic liberties and encourage you to do the same. It's better to create a design that you love than have a technically correct design that is a headache to create. Similarly, I've simplified the math and science explanations. People spend their entire lives studying these topics and becoming experts; I'm reducing that to a paragraph. Like with my middle school students, I'm hoping to instill enough curiosity in you that you'll look into some of these topics further.

Ali

Geometry

I love geometry. There, I said it. If you don't love it, I would guess it's because of those pesky area and perimeter calculations. Luckily, we don't need those. We just need to know our shapes and embrace their unique qualities.

One of the first things you are usually told in a beginning drawing course is that basic shapes—rectangles, triangles, circles, ovals—can be used to draw just about anything. The same shapes form our quilts. Looking at the most traditional quilts, we see designs such as Log Cabin and Courthouse Steps made from a square and rectangles. The Ohio Star combines squares and triangles. Flying Geese are just triangles. The Nine-Patch is made up of nine squares and the Drunkard's Path comprises quarter circles.

Rectangles

The rectangle is perhaps the most important shape we will be using. Because of the right angles, rectangles come together easily. And just so we're clear, the square is just a special rectangle that has four equal sides. These are going to be our building blocks. Even when we make blocks of other shapes, we will square them up before sewing them together. *Squaring up* means making the corners into right angles. **Figure A**

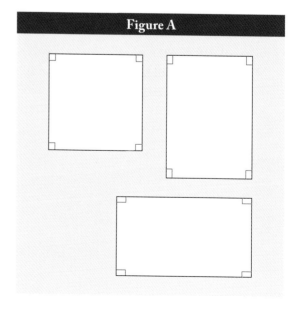

Figure A

Triangles

Triangles offer more variety than rectangles because the angles change. Triangles can be considered

- equilateral: all sides and angles have the same measure

- isosceles: two sides and two angles have the same measure

- scalene: no sides or angles have the same measure

No matter what kind of triangle you end up with, though, the three interior angles will always add up to 180°. **Figure B**

The most common triangle in quilting is the *isosceles right triangle*. With one right angle and two equal sides, these are often made by cutting a square in half along the diagonal. Some refer to these as half-square triangles (HSTs). Cutting a rectangle on the diagonal will result in a half-rectangle triangle (HRT). Because you still have the 90° angle but all of the sides are different lengths, this is a *scalene right triangle*. **Figure C**

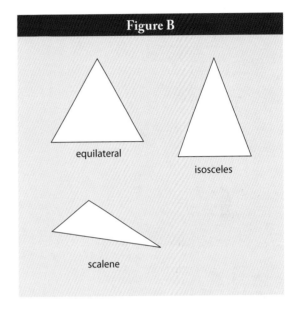

Figure B

equilateral

isosceles

scalene

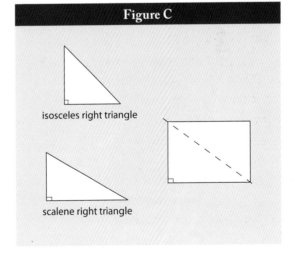

Figure C

isosceles right triangle

scalene right triangle

You may also remember something about the Pythagorean theorem—maybe just the name. This is used with right triangles (and HSTs) and comes in handy when you are trying to figure out side lengths and how big to make your blocks. I have included a handy table in the Appendix, but here's the formula in case you can't find the size you are looking for.

Formula: $a^2 + b^2 = c^2$

Sides *a* and *b* are always the two sides (called legs) that make the right angle; it's OK if you switch them. Side *c* is always the hypotenuse, or the longest side, opposite the right angle. **Figure D**

When you have to make many of the same HST block, it's quicker to start with a larger square, sew around the outside, and then cut the block into quarters. When you use this method, *c* (the hypotenuse) of your finished block will be the side length of your starting block. In this case you want to use the formula below, where *a* is the side length of your finished HST block and *c* is the side length of the square you should start with. It may look confusing, but just plug it into your phone or calculator and it'll do the hard part. *Remember, we always work in finished dimensions and then add ¼″ to each side for seam allowances at the end.* **Figure E**

Formula: $\sqrt{2a^2} = c$, **then add 1″ for seam allowances**

Isosceles triangles are perhaps the most versatile triangle in sewing. If you are making a shape composed of equal wedges—circles, pentagons, and starburst blocks trimmed down to squares—you'll be working with isosceles triangles. **Figure F**

Equilateral triangles are by far my favorite to sew. When you sew two together, you don't need to worry about offsetting them at all; just place one on top of the other and sew! We'll talk more about that when we get to the Angles chapter (page 66). These are used when sewing hexagons with six wedges.

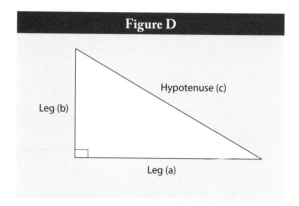

Figure D

Leg (b)

Hypotenuse (c)

Leg (a)

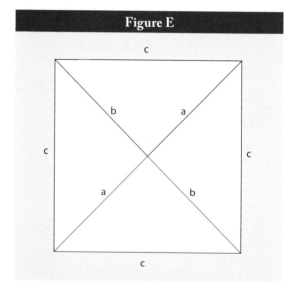

Figure E

c

b   a

c   c

a   b

c

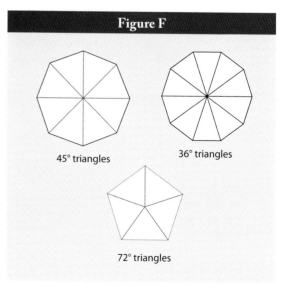

Figure F

45° triangles

36° triangles

72° triangles

Circles

The circle is one continuous line that has no beginning or end. The *diameter* is like the belt of the circle, going from edge to edge through the belly button. The *radius* is half of the diameter, going from the center to one edge. We'll be talking about the radius quite a bit when discussing how to cut the circles for quilts in this book. **Figure G**

It's also good to know that the interior angles of a circle add up to 360°. When we are creating wedges within a circle (or a hexagon or pentagon), we can calculate the angles we need. If you want 10 wedges in your circle, divide 360° by 10 and you know that the tip of each wedge should be 36°. See how this connects back to triangles? **Figure H**

Angles

For our purposes, it's important to know a little about how angles behave. Say you want a finished angle of 40°. When you tack on ¼″ seam allowances to each side, that angle will still be 40°. What changes is the length that the piece needs to be because you lose quite a bit of fabric at the tip to the seam allowance. You may notice that specialty angle rulers have the tip cut off because that bit is lost in the seam allowance and just creates bulk. **Figure I**

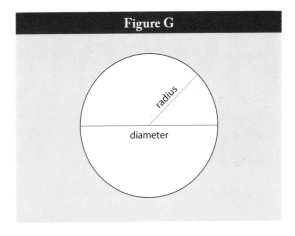

Figure G

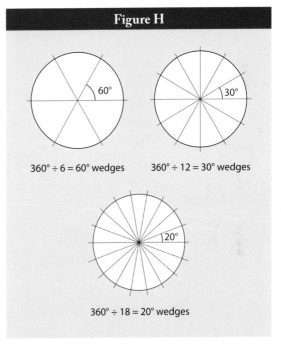

Figure H

360° ÷ 6 = 60° wedges   360° ÷ 12 = 30° wedges

360° ÷ 18 = 20° wedges

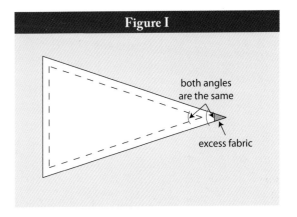

Figure I

Hypotenuten:
Shortcuts, Tips, and Tricks

When I was in college, I had a friend who called taking the shortcut "hypotenuten." I assure you that this is *very* geeky. The long side of a right triangle is called the hypotenuse (side *c*, remember?). Instead of walking the two sides that form a right angle, it's shorter to just cut across the diagonal. Thus *hypotenuten*.

Here are some of my favorite sewing shortcuts and some tips that should make your quilt come together faster.

Special Angles

You *do not* need lots of fancy angle rulers or square rulers unless they make you happy. Rotary rulers and cutting mats have a grid for a reason.

We can use this grid to make any angle using a concept called *slope*. Slope tells us how slanted a line is in the form of *rise* over *run*—go *up* this many units on a grid, then *over* that many units.

The following are the most common angles that you will use and how to create them. These angles are usually marked on larger cutting mats and rulers. However, it's nice to know how to create them should you not be able to see or use those premarked lines. I have also included a table in the Appendix (page 128) that shows a larger variety of slopes and their corresponding angles.

A 90° angle has no slope. It goes straight up and doesn't run to the side at all. The grid lines form 90° angles. **Figure A**

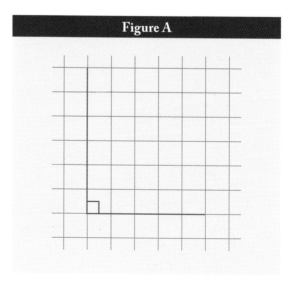

Figure A

A 45° angle is formed by going up one unit and over one unit. This angle is formed when you cut a square in half along the diagonal. Your ruler and cutting mat probably have this line marked. **Figure B**

A 30° angle is formed by going up four and over seven units. This actually creates a 29.7° angle; 0.3° is such a minor difference, especially in terms of sewing, that this should not create any issues in your piece. **Figure C**

A 60° angle is formed by going up seven and over four units. This actually creates a 60.25° angle. Like with the 30° angles, 0.25° is such a minor difference, especially in terms of sewing, that this should not create any issues in your piece. **Figure D**

Notice that the 30° and 60° angles use the same numbers, just flipped (4/7 and 7/4). They are *complementary angles*. When cutting your fabric, double-check that you are cutting the correct angle. If your cutting mat is upside down, you may find yourself using the 30° line to cut a 60° angle. This is true for all complementary angles.

marking tips

- I *adore* my washable marking pen. I have found that it works for all of my projects and has never failed to wash out or fade after a few hours (knock on wood!). I have also found that it will fade from my cutting mat as well. This is great for making marks for your current project.

- You can use washi tape or painter's tape to mark your rulers too if you are going to be cutting the same angle many times. When cutting the pieces for my *States of Matter* quilt (page 68), I marked the ruler with tape so that I didn't have to reposition the fabric on a marked cut line.

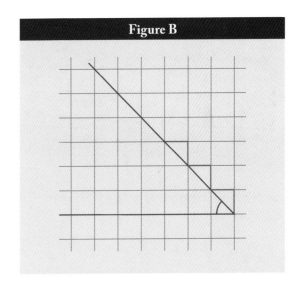

Figure B

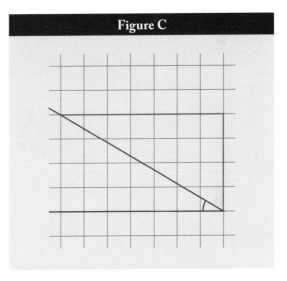

Figure C

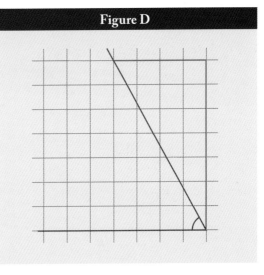

Figure D

Adjusting Your Seam Allowance

The quilting standard is a ¼˝ seam allowance. While some of the newer sewing machines come with a ¼˝ foot, I have found that it is not necessary; you can use the standard foot and adjust the needle position accordingly. Even if you use a ¼˝ foot, I would suggest checking your seams to make sure that they are accurate. Why? Because changing the needle size and thread brand can affect your seam allowance, albeit minimally.

To check for the correct needle position, you will need a scrap piece of fabric, ruler, pen, and sewing machine with the needle and thread you will be using.

Draw a line ¼˝ from the edge of the scrap of fabric. Now sew on this line. I like to use the edge of my presser foot and just scoot the needle over to the right until it sews along the line. You may need to try this a few times or make adjustments as you sew along the line until you find the sweet spot. Write down the needle position! **Figure E**

Chain Piecing

Chain piecing is a technique used in quilting to sew together many pieces continuously. To chain piece, sew one of your seams; when you get to the end, sew past the end a few stitches and place another piece of fabric beneath the presser foot (no need to lift it!). Keep going until you have sewn as many seams as needed. Some people like to leave a small piece of fabric in the machine to make starting the next chain easier. It's a great idea, but I always forget! **Figure F**

You should have a few stitches between each piece that you can cut apart. **Figure G**

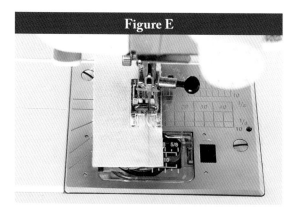

Figure E

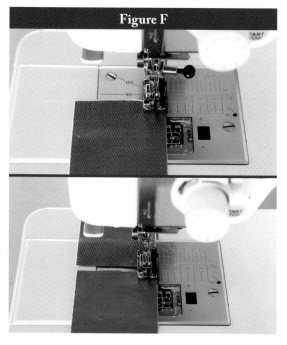

Figure F

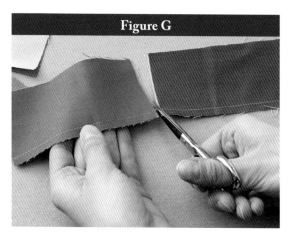

Figure G

Pressing Seams

Some people prefer to press their seams open; others prefer to press seams to one side. There isn't a "correct" way, and I change my pressing according to what I'm making.

I find that pressing seams open makes them pull apart more easily, and they are harder to line up. However, pressing seams open gives the finished piece the appearance of being a continuous piece, reduces bulk in seams, and makes quilting in-the-ditch much easier. **Figure H**

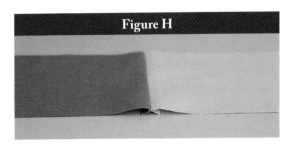

Pressing to one side creates a sort of bump. If you press seams in opposite directions, this bump allows the seams to "nest," making matching seams fairly easy and clean. **Figure I**

When nesting seams, I like to pin at a diagonal through both seams to hold them in place. I also take out the pin right before sewing over it to avoid accidentally hitting the pin with the needle or sewing in some distortion that the pin creates. **Figure J**

Another thing to consider when pressing seams is shrinkage. Pressing seams open means that the fabric is folding right on the seamline. When pressing to one side there is a bump where the fabric goes up and then over. While minute, that bump can mean losing more than ¼″ to the seam. Over multiple seams it adds up and can cause your block to be smaller than intended. To avoid this shrinkage press the seams open or cut the pieces ⅛″ wider, and trim as you go. **Figure K**

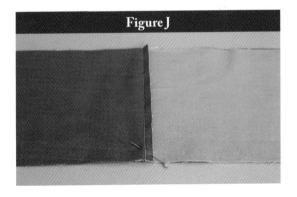

Regardless of pressing direction, I use a dry, hot iron when pressing seams. Place your iron down for a few seconds and resist the urge to move it around—that can create distortion. Let the piece cool before you pick it up. When I finish piecing a block or row, especially one with a lot of seams, I give it a good steamy press, let it cool, and then set it aside flat or hang it until I use it in the final assembly.

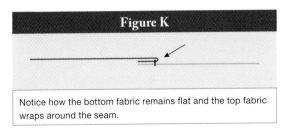

Notice how the bottom fabric remains flat and the top fabric wraps around the seam.

Washing

Prewashing fabric is in *no way* a shortcut. It takes time and is not usually necessary. The fabric frays in the wash and has to be cut apart. If you don't get the fabric out of the dryer immediately, then you will become fast friends with your iron. Some people choose to prewash because

- It shrinks the fabric so that the final quilt shrinks less. **Figure L**

- If the colors are going to run, then they won't ruin any other fabrics.

- They want to remove the chemicals used to make new fabrics stiff and glossy.

It's more important to prewash fabric for garments so that you get the right fit. Flannel tends to shrink more than quilting cotton, so if I am using this for quilt backing I wash it first.

Batting can also be prewashed. I have *never* prewashed batting, but batting shrinks too, especially if you are using 100% cotton or a blend with a high percentage of cotton. I think that the shrinkage of batting creates a crinkly charm to the end quilt, which is how I justify skipping this step.

Design Wall

I have a king-size flannel sheet hanging on my wall with push pins—definitely *not* fancy, but it does the job. Design walls are a great place to put your pieces as you work on them to see how things are coming together. You want to aim for a space that has plenty of light and room for you to back away and see the whole thing. If that isn't in your sewing area, just think of the extra exercise you'll get going back and forth as well as the changing art that your other space will be graced with!

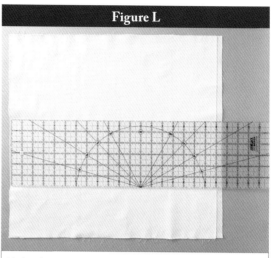

Figure L

Notice that the fabric shrunk ½" in one direction and not at all in the other direction.

Note

My husband is always surprised by how small the quilts are when they are finished. Between the design wall and sewing the quilt top together, you will lose quite a few inches. Remember that for each seam you will lose ½". Because you'll be planning your quilts based on the final dimensions, rest assured that you will end up with a quilt that's the size you want (no matter how big it looks on the design wall).

Essential Tools

For designing

1. Graph paper

2. Pens and pencils

3. Eraser

4. Colored pencils

5. Small ruler

6. Protractor

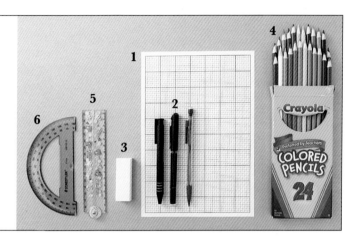

For sewing

1. Rotary ruler—3″ × 18″ or 6″ × 24″

2. Rotary cutter (45mm) and mat

3. Needles: Sizes 9–11 for piecing, 14–16 for quilting

4. Seam ripper

5. Thread

6. Pins

7. Iron and ironing board

8. Scissors

9. Sewing machine with basic stitches

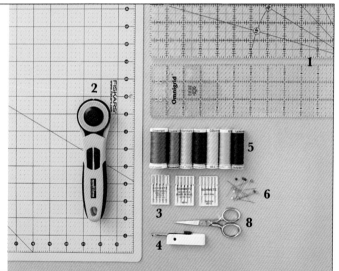

Have handy

1. Washi and Scotch tape

2. Bamboo skewer or chopstick

3. Gluestick

4. Freezer paper

5. Washable-ink pen

Design Process

I have taken some artistic liberties to make the designs easier to piece and to translate them into graphic quilts. Remember to have fun with the process and not get too caught up in making an exact replica of your inspiration. It's the flow of the design process that will lead you to a perfectly unique quilt.

The Scientific Method

All science experiments follow the same process:

- An experiment starts with a question: What do you want to know?

- Next, research the subject about which you have the question.

- Then form a hypothesis: Based on what you know, what do you think you will find out? What will be the answer or the result, or what will happen?

- The experiment is performed.

- Finally, what did your results show? Was your hypothesis correct?

While these steps don't apply to quilting, they do help us to understand that science experiments always involve a process, whether explicit or implied. Likewise, every quilt also goes through a process. Below I have outlined the steps that I take in my quiltmaking process. You may want to tweak these steps to work better for you, but you should always start with inspiration and end with an amazing quilt!

Step 1: Inspiration

Inspiration can come from anywhere. I find that mine usually comes from my students or right before I fall asleep—when I'm feeling too lazy to turn on a light and write it down.

Color inspiration is everywhere—from clothing and fashion to nature. Look at paint colors, your favorite item of clothing, advertisements in magazines, or even your favorite website. Maybe a bunch of balloons or a paint sample will inspire you, or maybe the selvage of your favorite fabric. Squint your eyes when you look at things, or take a picture with your camera out of focus to get a better idea of the colors and shapes. Also several websites are available where you can upload a picture to find the color palette used.

The quilts in this book have been abstracted from math and science principles, but I have found inspiration for quilts everywhere—in rug patterns, wallpaper, fabrics, website designs, and even accidental stacks of fabric. I suggest keeping a small inspiration board—physical, digital, or both—to help you keep track of your ideas.

Step 2: Plan

Some people can visualize what they want their quilt to look like and just make it come to life. I have found that I need a bit more structure to my process. I like to plan and make lists. I also like to make sure I have my calculations correct before I cut into my precious fabric.

Small Sketches

Start small. I start with a small square (about 2″ × 2″) and draw what is considered a thumbnail sketch. This allows me to make lots of drawings quickly and decide what scale each of the components should be. You can't fit in much detail on a thumbnail sketch, but it's like looking at your quilt from afar and getting a sense of the overall design. **Figure A**

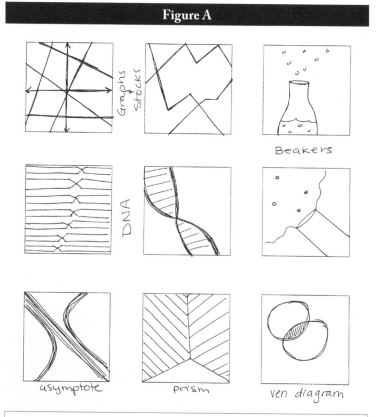

Figure A

I started off sketching ideas for any science concept that popped into my mind. These are some of the designs that didn't make the cut for this book.

Add Details

Now work out the details on graph paper. Draw a large rectangle on the page (or square if you want a square quilt). It should take up about 75% of the page, leaving room for adjustments to the size and for notes. Select the thumbnail sketch(es) that you like and draw the design in the rectangle. You don't need to be precise yet. Right now you're getting a better idea of the design and where each element should be. This is the time to add details that you didn't have room for in the thumbnail sketch. Work with the lines on your graph paper; use them to help you determine the design size and angles. Make notes about ideas you have for colors or construction.

What Size?

How big is your quilt going to be? Baby size, lap size, bed size? Just get an idea right now, not the precise dimensions. Your quilt design will dictate exactly how big the quilt ends up. I like a large lap quilt that I can use on the couch or throw on the bed at night as an extra layer on my side of the bed. Most of the quilts in this book are lap quilts to make them less overwhelming, but it's easy to change the size of the blocks to make a larger or smaller quilt.

When you know how big you want your quilt, figure out a scale for the graph-paper sketch. Divide the desired width (in inches) by how many squares wide the sketch is, and that will tell you how many inches each square represents. Repeat for the length. Note the scale on the graph paper. For example, I wanted my quilt to be 40″ wide; I had drawn the sketch 12 squares wide. This would make each square represent 3.33333″. In the final revision, you may decide to make each box represent 3″, but you would end up with a 36″ quilt. To end up with the desired 40″ quilt, you will have to draw your final design 10 boxes wide so that each represents 4″.

Always draw your quilt in finished dimensions. For example, if you are using charm squares (5″ squares that finish to 4½″ squares), you will want to make each square on your graph paper equal 4½″. Jelly roll strips finish to 2″ wide, so each square should equal 2″. If you aren't using precuts, think about the desired size of the quilt and how much detail you want.

Note

Although you have a scale, it can change at any time. Think of this as a fluid process. Maybe you started with a lap quilt but now you want a bed quilt. All you have to do is change the scale and make the blocks bigger. Instead of the squares representing 2″, they now equal 3″, making the quilt just slightly larger. Jump up to 5″ and the quilt will be quite a bit larger, or scale down to 1″ for a mini-quilt.

Final Draft

Now that you have a scale and larger design to work from, take a new piece of graph paper and draw the bounding box (resized from the previous one if necessary). You will want to use a dark pencil or pen, ruler, and protractor if you are creating angles. Add the design, being as precise as possible and making any adjustments as you go.

This is the point when I head to my computer and draw the design in Adobe Illustrator or AutoCAD. I know others who use Microsoft Excel, Electric Quilt, or Microsoft Word. You don't need to invest in expensive programs to design beautiful quilts though. **Figure B**

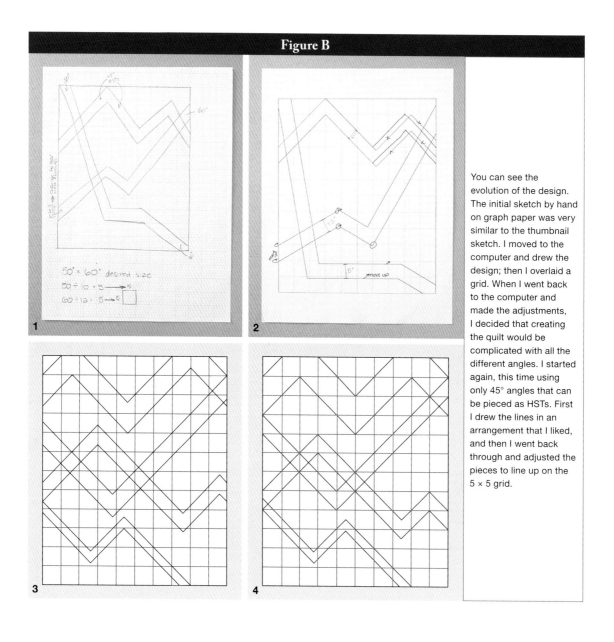

Figure B

You can see the evolution of the design. The initial sketch by hand on graph paper was very similar to the thumbnail sketch. I moved to the computer and drew the design; then I overlaid a grid. When I went back to the computer and made the adjustments, I decided that creating the quilt would be complicated with all the different angles. I started again, this time using only 45° angles that can be pieced as HSTs. First I drew the lines in an arrangement that I liked, and then I went back through and adjusted the pieces to line up on the 5 × 5 grid.

Make Copies

Take your ink design and make at least five photocopies. I like to place my originals in a page-protector sleeve in a binder. I try out different color options on the copies and use them to make notes about piecing and seams. It's nice to always have the original to go back to in case you need to make more copies. When I'm finished, I put all the pages with notes in the sleeve with the original.

Boxed Up

Using your photocopies, figure out how the quilt will be assembled. If you are using nonrectangular shapes, give each shape a bounding box. Because your design is on graph paper it should be fairly easy to create a grid, but you may need to stagger the blocks or create blocks of different sizes to accommodate the design. These boxes will allow you to visualize how the pieces will fit together and should form a grid, columns or rows, or quadrants. Remember that you also can assemble rows and columns of blocks set on point, so look along the diagonals as well for a possible assembly grid. If you can't find a grid, smaller squares and rectangles should form a few larger rectangles that can then be sewn together to create the final quilt top. *Scattered* (page 58) and *Cultured* (page 104) are great examples of how I break different designs into chunks that can be easily pieced together.

Within your larger blocks you may also need to break down the piecing of smaller blocks. If you have a lot of detail or small pieces, you can draw each block at a larger scale on another piece of graph paper. After the block is drawn, repeat the process of breaking the block into a grid or rectangles that can be assembled into rows, columns, or quadrants.

Cutting List

Now that you have all the boxes and a general assembly diagram, figure out the pieces that you will need. Remember that the seam allowances are *not* yet included. *You will need to add ¼″ to each side of each shape.* For nonrectangular shapes, I tend to cut my pieces a bit larger and then trim them down. This creates slightly more waste but more precise pieces. I write the dimensions directly on a copy of my boxed-up quilt design, but you could create a list by color.

Step 3: Pull Fabrics

This is the fun part for many of us. While the inspiration, design, and color plan should help you decide what prints work best, keep in mind a few things:

- Large prints won't show in small pieces.

- Solids or tone-on-tone prints give the eye a place to rest.

- Play with the color wheel to find combinations that you may not be familiar with.

- Pick a few different combinations and photograph them, and then see if one set stands out among the pictures.

Step 4: Cut

You may want to cut everything at once, or you may look at the design and decide to cut only the pieces for one small section at a time. Both methods have advantages—saving time versus knowing exactly where each piece goes. Choose what works best for you and the design. If you cut all the pieces at once, use tape and a pen to mark the pieces and write down your key on one of the photocopies.

Step 5: Lay Things Out

After the pieces are cut out, take them to your design board. Do you still like the fabrics you have chosen? Does the arrangement work? Take a picture to help you see the overall design and if there are any spots that aren't working. Seeing a small thumbnail of the design on your camera, phone, or computer will show you if some fabrics stand out too much or if the colors are distributed evenly. Now is the time to play around and find the right composition. Make sure you take a quick picture of the final layout to reference in case your pieces get mixed up.

Step 6: Sew

Start sewing your pieces together according to your design, using a ¼″ seam allowance. How you press seams is a personal preference (page 13). As you piece parts together, place them on a design wall to get an idea of how they are coming together, to keep them in the right place, and to get a sense of accomplishment!

No matter how you prefer to design, by hand or by machine, the process stays the same: inspiration, design, turn design into a workable quilt, pick colors and fabric, and sew!

My Quilt-Finishing Method

This is the part that slows me down. I love the design process, playing with fabric, and seeing my designs come to life. The sandwiching, quilting, and binding are necessary evils for me. Many options and methods are available for each step. I'm going to cover the methods that I use and have had luck with. For a refresher on finishing quilts, check out C&T Publishing's tips and techniques at tinyurl.com/quiltmaking-basics.

Quilt Backs

You can be so creative in how you piece the back, but I struggle with the idea of making another quilt just to put on the back. Do quilts really need to be reversible? In the end I try to use a large piece of fabric and piece the back as little as possible. This is getting easier as more fabric designs are manufactured in 108″ widths. Sometimes inspiration strikes and I do piece the back to coordinate with the front. I have included piecing directions for my "inspired" quilt backs in the book. I've included fabric requirements should you want to use my directions or go wholecloth. Feel free to piece any and all the quilt backs to your heart's content! Look for coordinating scraps or fabrics that fit the science theme, or pull out those pieces that you just need to use up.

Batting

- If you purchase batting that's rolled up in a bag, open it up and smooth it out a day in advance to loosen up the wrinkles.

- Most cotton batting has been needle punched to make it easier to quilt. This process also gives the batting a right side and wrong side. The wrong side looks like fluffy clouds, and you can't see individual needle holes. This side will go next to your quilt back. The right side has little needle holes in it and will go next to the quilt top. This allows your needle to go through the materials easier, prolonging the life of the needle. **Figure A**

- Make sure that at least 2″ of batting extends beyond each side of the quilt. The quilt back should be approximately the same size as the batting. **Figure B**

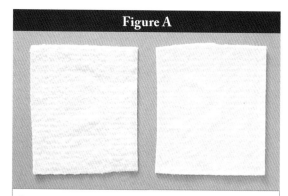
Figure A

On the right you see the right side, and on the left you see the wrong side. Notice that there is more of a visible pattern from the needle punching on the piece on the right.

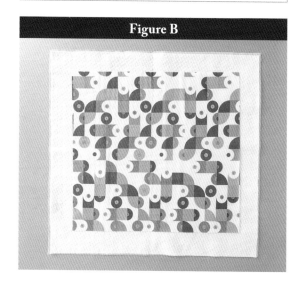
Figure B

Sandwiching

I tried putting the layers together with safety pins, but our carpeted apartment was not conducive to that method. I bought a quilting frame and tried basting the layers together with large stitches. This was better but time consuming, and I still found puckers in my final pieces. I finally tried spray basting and have not looked back! You do have to do this outside, or in a space with very good ventilation.

Lay the quilt backing on a firm surface, wrong side up. Smooth out any wrinkles, then place the batting right side up on the backing. Finally, smooth down the quilt top right side up. Peel back the quilt top and apply the glue to the batting, following the directions on the can. Use long strokes about 8″ away from the batting. Start in the center and work your way out to the sides and corners. For baby and lap quilts, I have found that working in halves is great. For larger quilts, I fold back half of the quilt top or back, but only spray half of the exposed batting, essentially working in quarters. Working with smaller sections will help you avoid puckers and makes the project much more manageable.

Quilting

- I like straight-line quilting. It's fairly easy, especially with a walking foot, but can be time consuming depending on how close the lines are.

- I draw the quilting pattern I'm considering on one of the photocopies of my design (page 21) to make sure I like how the two go together.

- When free-motion or straight-line quilting, you will want larger stitches. I set my stitch length between a 4.0 and 4.5 when I straight-line quilt. The larger stitches make the quilting go faster and are easier to rip out if you make a mistake. **Figure C**

- The denser the quilting is, the stiffer the quilt will be. Check the rating on your batting to see the maximum distance apart recommended for quilting lines. Depending on the brand and fiber, you can have fairly large open spaces.

- When trimming off the excess batting and backing after quilting, I trim two sides with scissors; then I fold the quilt into quarters and trim the other sides with my rotary cutter to make sure that everything is square.

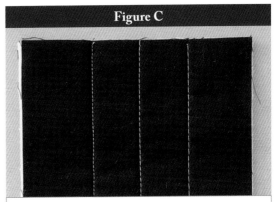

Figure C

On the left the stitch length is 2.5—what I use for piecing. The middle line is stitched at 3.5, and the one on the right is 4.5.

Binding

I make all binding using 2½″ strips cut on the straight grain—as opposed to bias. This binding will end up being about ⅜″ wide when finished. If you prefer a narrower binding, cut your strips 2″. Unless you are sewing a small project, I don't recommend going smaller than 2″. If you want a more visible binding (to create more of a border or frame), 3″ or 3½″ strips work great. **Figure D**

To calculate how much binding you will need, measure the perimeter of your quilt, then divide

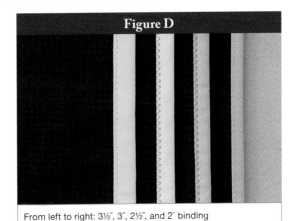

Figure D

From left to right: 3½″, 3″, 2½″, and 2″ binding

by 37. This is a slight overestimate. Your answer is how many 2½″ × WOF (width of fabric) strips you will need.

Formula: perimeter / 37 = number of strips

To calculate how much yardage of the binding fabric to buy, multiply the number of strips by your binding width—usually 2½″. For most lap quilts, ½ yard of fabric for binding is enough.

Formula: number of strips × 2.5 = number of inches of fabric

After all your strips are cut, assemble them with diagonal seams into one long strip of usable binding. Fold and press in half lengthwise.

Did I mention that binding is not my favorite part? I have friends who love binding and beg me to let them bind my quilts. I really do have the best friends. But I digress. To make it more tolerable and faster, I have quite a few machine binding gadgets, and I sew 99% of my binding completely by machine. I love using a zigzag stitch to finish the binding because it's much more forgiving than a straight stitch.

Labeling

After investing hours upon hours in your quilts, take credit for the work! Traditional quilt labels include name, location, and date. You may want to put a message to the recipient. You can embroider, use fabric pens, or digitally print them. I have seen people use a certain fabric in the binding as a signature, or sew a block into the back of the quilt with their information.

I prefer a combination of methods. I created a 3″ × 3″ label on the computer with care instructions and my logo and had it professionally printed on fabric. I fold that in half along the diagonal and sew it onto the back in the lower left corner when I sew on the binding. I write in the date when I finish the quilt. Sometimes, I mark that corner with a different fabric than the rest of the binding. **Figure E**

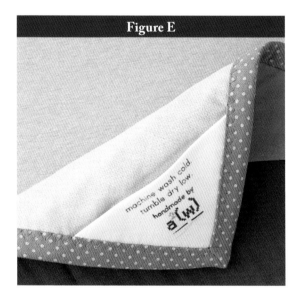

Figure E

Small Projects

I have put together a few small projects that are less time consuming than quilts and can be useful in your daily routines.

The first project is a small notebook. I make these with graph paper and keep them in my purse and by my bed for jotting down quilt ideas (or figuring out how to build something, or ideas for lessons). With plain paper they are great sketchbooks. You could also print coloring-book pages to make an inexpensive and personalized kids' activity.

The pillow and the tote are ways to put mini-quilts to use. Create a coordinating pillow for your bed or couch. Or create a matching gift or storage bag for a quilt. These small projects are a fun way to bring your quilting ideas to life with less of a time investment. Spruce up your home or an outfit with a personal touch that you can appreciate even when you can't be snuggled up under a quilt.

Pocket Sketchbook

-------------------- Finished size: 8½" × 5½" --------------------------------

I have made dozens of these little guys. Because they are so simple and cheap, I have dedicated ones for different uses. I have one with graph paper for my quilt sketches. Another is for quick notes and lists. Plain printer paper is great to use for drawing and sketches or for kids to color and scribble. These sketchbooks can be made in many sizes; they are light, and they are super easy to throw into your bag so that you're always ready to capture your next great idea.

Materials

Cardstock: 8½˝ × 11˝

Paper: 12 sheets 8½˝ × 11˝ (lined, graph, or plain)

Print fabric: 9½˝ × 12˝

Needle, size 14

4 binder clips or large paperclips

Wax paper

Mod Podge (all-in-one glue, sealer, and finish)

1˝-wide bristle paint brush

tips

- I have found that these little books do best with 12 pages of paper. Unless your paper is thin, like newsprint, sewing more layers can be difficult and makes the book harder to close.

- For the cardstock I use magazine boards because I also use them for mini fabric bolts. Cereal boxes and 4-ply Bristol Vellum are also an appropriate weight.

Make It!

1. Score the center of the outside of the cardstock lightly with a rotary cutter or X-Acto knife. Fold the cardstock in half so that it measures 8½″ × 5½″, crease firmly, and then open.

2. Fold the paper in half so it measures 8½″ × 5½″. To get a nice crease and for accuracy, fold no more than 3 pages at a time.

3. Align the folds on the paper and cardstock. Clip all layers together. **Figure A**

4. Set the stitch length to a basting length (I use a stitch length of 4).

5. With a size 14 needle and the pages facing up, sew on the fold line. I use a pencil to lightly mark the crease so that it's easier to see when sewing. Leave the ends of the thread long.

6. Open the notebook flat with the cardstock facing up. Knot the ends of the threads; then glue them to the cardstock. **Figure B**

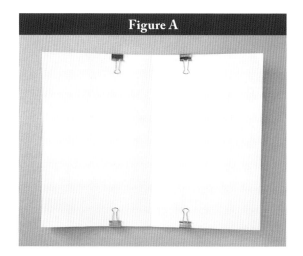

Figure A

Figure B

7. Fold the notebook in half. Starting at the outside edge, cover half of the back cover with Mod Podge. Center the fabric and smooth in place. Because the fabric is larger, you don't have to be exact. Peel back the fabric and glue down the other half nearest the spine. Press.

8. Flip the book over, keeping it closed. Starting at the spine, glue the fabric to the book cover. **Figure C**

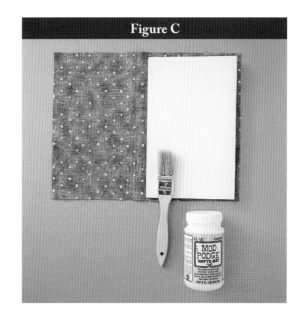

Figure C

9. Cover the fabric with a piece of wax paper on both sides; then place the notebook under a heavy book. Let dry for 4 or more hours.

10. With the notebook open and the pages facing up, trim off the excess fabric from the top and bottom. Try not to cut the thread. **Figure D**

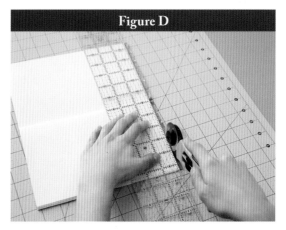

Figure D

11. Fold the notebook along the seam and press. Trim the excess fabric and cardboard at the opening so that the cover is the same size as the pages within. You may want to trim the pages as well to even them out. **Figure E**

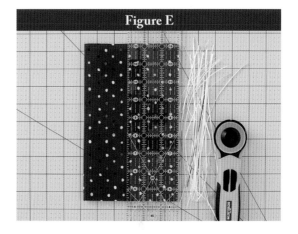

Figure E

Pillow Perfect

-------------- Finished size: 24″ × 24″ --------------

Neutrals, such as white walls, white couches, and white sheets, are the perfect backdrop for colorful accessories like pillows and quilts that are easily changed out with your mood or the season. Quilted pillows are a great way to bring a design into a room, but still encourage friends to get cozy. Pillows also let you experiment with color, design, and quilting patterns.

When scaling your design down to pillow size, keep in mind standard pillow form sizes and how small your pieces will become. Pillow forms are generally square, although rectangular and round options are available. I have used square forms in rectangular pillow covers without any problems—just make sure the pillow form isn't too firm and that you buy a size that matches the longest side of your pillow cover.

> **tip**
>
> Although it may seem counterintuitive, plan for the unfinished pillow cover to have the same dimensions as the pillow form. Do not add in any seam allowances around the outside; that will create a fuller pillow. For example, for a 24″ × 24″ pillow form, your unfinished quilt top should be 24″ × 24″.

If you have an intricate design, the pieces will become quite small. You may wish to foundation piece them or take some detail out of your design.

For pillows, I follow the same steps as with quilts. Creating mini-quilt sandwiches is satisfying because of how quickly they come together and because I can use up scraps of batting. I back my mini-quilt sandwiches with either muslin or fabric that I no longer want; this will be on the inside of the pillow cover.

This pillow features an envelope closure and a bound edge. Finishing the pillow with a binding eliminates raw edges, reduces bulk on the interior of the pillow, and gives the impression of piping.

The design is the same as the large *Fractal* quilt (page 50) but uses squares instead of the same-color Four-Patch blocks.

Materials

For the fractal mini-quilt

Orange: 1 square 1½″ × 1½″

Gray: fat quarter

Green: fat quarter

Aqua: fat quarter

Navy: ⅜ yard

Peach: 2 squares 8½″ × 8½″

Backing: 27″ × 27″

Batting: 27″ × 27″

For the pillow

Back fabric: ¾ yard

Binding: ⅓ yard

Pillow form: 24″ × 24″

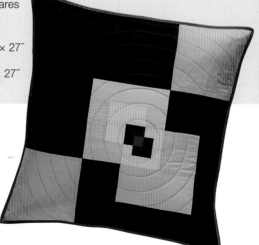

Cut It!

WOF = width of fabric

GRAY

- 1 strip 1½″ × 20″: Subcut into 6 squares 1½″ × 1½″.

GREEN

- 1 strip 2½″ × 20″: Subcut into 3 squares 2½″ × 2½″.
- 1 strip 1½″ × 20″: Subcut into 9 squares 1½″ × 1½″.

AQUA

- 1 strip 4½″ × 20″: Subcut into 3 squares 4½″ × 4½″.
- 2 strips 2½″ × 20″: Subcut into 9 squares 2½″ × 2½″.

NAVY

- 1 strip 8½″ × WOF: Subcut into 3 squares 8½″ × 8½″.
- 1 strip 4½″ × WOF: Subcut into 9 squares 4½″ × 4½″.

BINDING

- 3 strips 2½″ × WOF.

Make It!

1. Assemble the mini-quilt according to the diagram. Baste and quilt as desired; then trim to 24″ × 24″. **Figure A**

2. You will need 2 pieces for the pillow back. To figure out their size, use the following formulas:

   width = same width as mini-quilt

   length = mini-quilt length × 2 ÷ 3 + 2 (Solve from left to right: multiply, then divide, then add. Order matters.)

For a 24″ × 24″ pillow form, each piece will measure 24″ × 18″:

   (24 × 2 = 48 ÷ 3 = 16 + 2 = 18 (length))

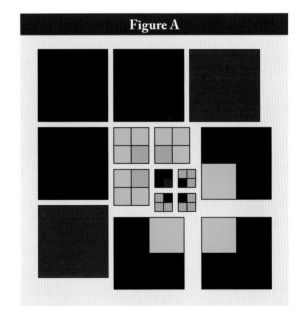

Figure A

3. On one backing piece, fold under ½˝ toward the wrong side of the fabric along the 24˝ edge. Press. Fold over 1˝, press, and sew ⅛˝ from each folded edge. Repeat on the other backing piece. **Figure B**

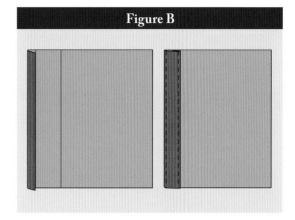

Figure B

> **tip**
>
> When I fold under edges—such as for pillows, garments, and bags—I always mark a "fold to" line that is twice the called-for width. For these folds, I mark 1˝ away from the edge (double my desired ½˝ width) and fold up to that line while I am pressing. Then I mark 2˝ from the new edge (again, double my desired 1˝ width) and fold up to that line.

4. Lay the mini-quilt with the back facing up. Align one backing piece along the bottom edge of the quilt, wrong side down and with the folded side in the middle of the quilt. Align the other backing piece along the top edge of the quilt, wrong side down. It should overlap the other piece by at least 4˝. Pin and baste around the outside with a ⅛˝ seam allowance. **Figure C**

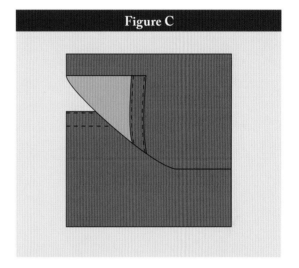

Figure C

5. Cut the binding strips 2½˝. Prepare the binding according to the directions on pages 25 and 26.

6. Sew the binding to the mini-quilt top using a ¼˝ seam allowance. Wrap the binding around to the back. Pin and machine or hand stitch down.

Back of pillow

School Tote

--------- **Finished size:** 12″ wide × 15″ tall × 3″ deep • **Finished block size:** 3″ × 3″ ---------

I've noticed that my students don't carry backpacks and that teachers don't allow backpacks in class. While I'm a bit baffled by this trend, it does create opportunities to use smaller and more unique bags. Students carry their supplies for a couple of classes at a time and use their lockers, so their bags don't have to be very big. Keeping in mind school supplies, I think this is an ideal size for a school tote. Of course, you could scale this pattern up to something larger to travel with or smaller for little kids.

Durability is an important feature in bags, more so than in pillows and quilts; bags carry heavy loads, are slung around daily, and are often placed on the ground. For larger bags, batting and quilting offer structure and design, but for small bags like this they create too much bulk. Instead, these directions call for backing your pieced mini-quilt (it's a mini-quilt before it's a bag!) with a light-weight interfacing and forgoing the batting and quilting altogether. The interfacing sets the seams and provides structure without much weight. If you love the look of quilting, you can always add it to your mini-quilt after interfacing the wrong side.

I've designed this bag to incorporate a few details that I love. You could make the handles out of fabric, but I really don't enjoy that part. I have found some fabulous cotton webbing options out there that look just as nice. I've also decided to round the corners of the bag so that we don't have to deal with gussets or boxing corners. The curve detail also takes the bag up a step from a simple tote. The last detail is using binding to finish the bag instead of turning everything inside out then right side out. The binding along the edges makes the bag reversible since all seams are finished.

Materials

For the mini-quilts

Beige: ¾ yard

Coral: 8 fat quarters of assorted prints

For the tote

Lining: ⅝ yard

Binding: 1 fat quarter

Lightweight fusible interfacing: 1 yard

1¼″-wide cotton webbing: 1¼ yards

Back of tote

Cut It!

WOF = width of fabric

Mini-Quilt

BEIGE

- 3 strips 4″ × WOF: Subcut into 64 wedges using pattern *b*. If using a print, cut with the fabric folded to yield mirror-images pieces.

- 2 strips 3½″ × WOF: Subcut 1 strip into 8 squares 3½″ × 3½″; trim the other strip to 3½″ × 39⅝″.

CORAL

- 1 strip from each print 3½″ × 20″: Subcut each strip into 4 triangles using pattern *a*.

Tote

LINING

- 1 strip 12½″ × WOF: Subcut into 2 rectangles 12½″ × 15½″.

- 1 strip 3½″ × WOF: Trim to 3½″ × 39⅝″.

BINDING

Since the edges are curved, the fabric must be cut on the bias.

- Fold fabric along the diagonal and cut along the fold.

- From the trimmed edge, cut 4 strips 2″ wide (lengths will vary). **Figure A**

INTERFACING

- 2 strips 11½″ × WOF: Subcut into 2 rectangles 11½″ × 14½″.

- 2 strips 2¾″ × WOF.

WEBBING

- Drape length across 1 shoulder and pull both ends to the opposite hip. Trim excess at hip.

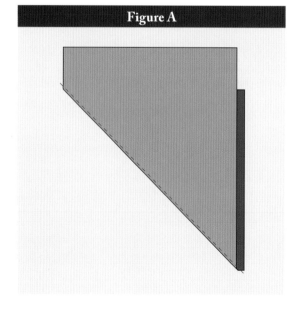

Figure A

Make It!

1. Assemble the mini-quilts according to the directions for *States of Matter* on page 68 and the diagrams. I have modified the design to have 5 rows instead of 9 and only 4 blocks per row, but the piecing will be the same. Trim blocks to 3½″ × 3½″. **Figure B**

2. Approximately center the 11½″ × 14½″ pieces of interfacing on the wrong sides of your mini-quilts. Press according to manufacturer's directions.

3. Place 1 piece of 2¾″ interfacing on the wrong side of the beige 3½″ × 39⅝″ strip. Place the interfacing ½″ from one end and centered along the width. Press according to the manufacturer's directions. Repeat with the other piece of interfacing at the other end. The pieces will overlap in the middle by a few inches.

4. Mark the centers of the interfaced strip along the length and width. Center and pin one end of the webbing along the width of the right side of the strip. Repeat on the other end, making sure not to twist the webbing. If your strap is shorter than 40″, the fabric will bow slightly.

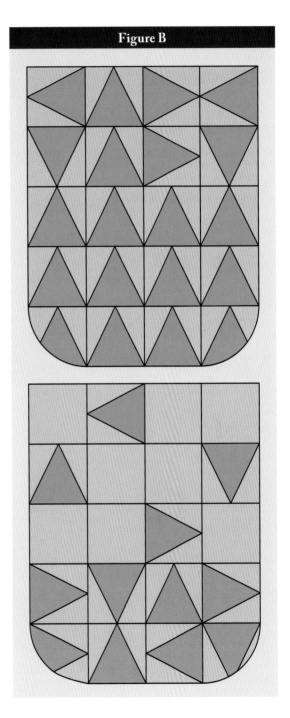

Figure B

5. With right sides together, sew the lining strip to the interfaced strip along the 3½˝ ends with a ½˝ seam, backstitching over the webbing to reinforce the seam. Turn right side out, press, and topstitch the ends. The fabric strips and webbing will form a circle. Baste along the 2 long open edges with a ⅛˝ seam allowance. **Figure C**

6. With right sides together, sew the lining pieces to the mini-quilt pieces along the top only. Turn right side out, press, and topstitch along the sewn edge. Baste along the 3 open edges with a ⅛˝ seam allowance.

7. Mark the curved corners on the bottom edges of the 2 panels using the corner pattern; then trim. You can use the included pattern or a compass. The center of the circle should be 3˝ from the side and bottom.

8. With the lining pieces facing, pin the center strip to one panel, aligning the tops and bottom middle. Pin the straight sides and bottom first and then pin the curves. It's easier to sew with the strip facing up. Baste with a ⅛˝ seam allowance. Repeat with the other panel. **Figure D**

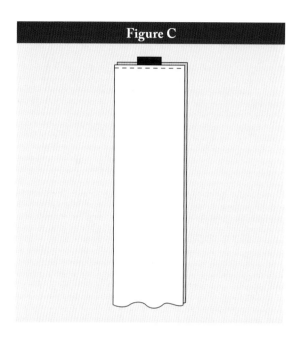

Figure C

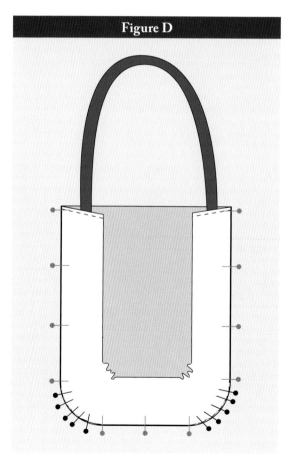

Figure D

9. Sew the binding pieces together according to the directions on pages 25 and 26. Cut into 2 pieces 39⅝″.

10. Unfold the binding and fold under ½″ at each end of the strips. Press.

11. With the folded edges at the top of the bag, pin the binding to one of the exposed seams, aligning the raw edges. Sew through all the layers with a scant ¼″ seam allowance. Fold over the binding and hand or machine sew to the other side. Repeat with the other piece of binding on the other side. **Figure E**

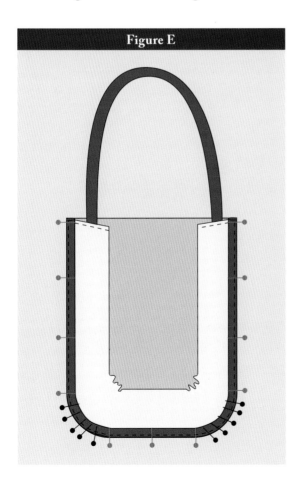

Figure E

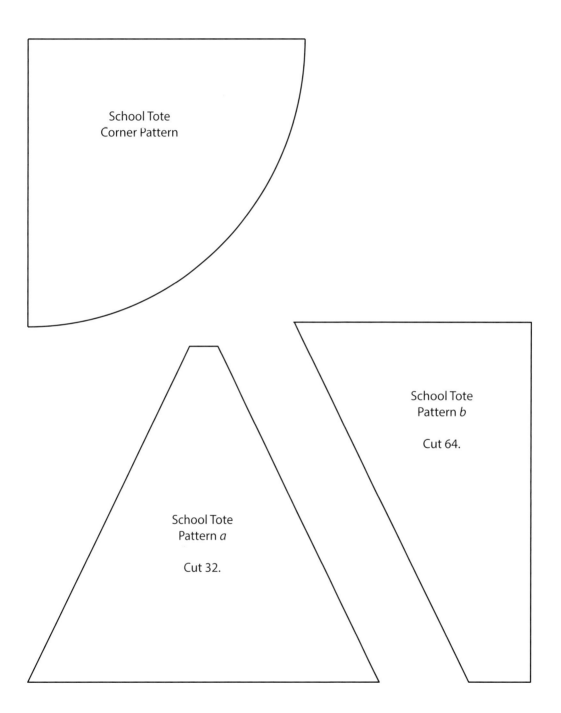

School Tote
Corner Pattern

School Tote
Pattern *b*

Cut 64.

School Tote
Pattern *a*

Cut 32.

Rectangles

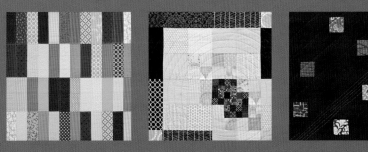

No matter what your skill level, sometimes it's nice to work on a simple project that doesn't involve angles or circles. These quilts provide visual interest and meaning, without requiring any complicated measurements or seams. As in each section, these quilts start off with basic piecing skills and work their way up to be a bit more complicated.

Basic Binary eases you into sewing together rectangles and details all of the steps that go into quilt construction—from layout to seam alignment and all the adjustments that happen along the way. *Fractal* shows you how to take a design and "chunk" it into smaller squares and rectangles that can then be assembled. *Scattered* is a little more complex, with smaller pieces and random placement.

Basic Binary

Finished quilt size: 40″ × 52½″ • Finished block size: 2½″ × 7½″

Inspiration

This quilt is based on binary code. What I love about this is the idea of ordered randomness. I'm terrible about just putting pieces in random places—I fuss, and in the end everything looks too planned, so using binary code to dictate color placement gives me boundaries to work within and adhere to. The blocks appear to have randomness, but they are in fact quite structured and intentional.

Planning

For this quilt, I've opted for warm and cool tones. Warm tones will mean 1s; cool tones will mean 0s. You could use any color combination—monochromatic with lights and darks of one shade, two different complementary colors, prints and solids, and so on.

Because each letter, number, and character has 7 digits, we will need to plan our quilt accordingly. Instead of going to graph paper and outlining a desired size, I just assigned each number a box, creating a 7 × 16 grid. From there I decided that I wanted the quilt to be approximately 40″ × 55″. I divided 40″ (the width) by 16 (the number of characters in my message), which equals 2½″ for the finished block width. For the height I divided 55″ by 7, which equals 7.857 and is an irrational number (also known as an "ugly number" in my classroom). I decided to round down to 7½″. (Remember, these are the finished dimensions.)

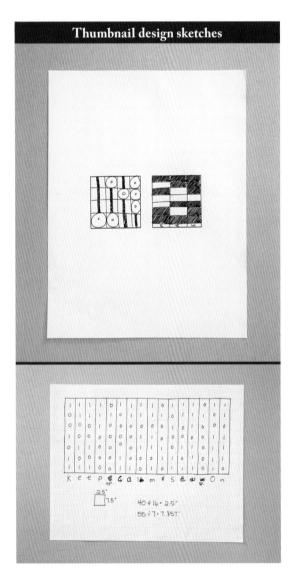

Thumbnail design sketches

Skills

This quilt should help you figure out how you prefer to line up seams. Do you press to one side and nest the seams, or do you press open and visually align them? When lining up this many seams I prefer to press to one side because it makes lining them up faster.

tip

Columns versus rows: Which seams do you sew first? I like to align as few seams as possible at the end, so I start where there are fewer seams. This quilt has 15 seams in each row, so if you sewed in rows, you would have to align all 15 seams when you sew the rows together. This quilt has half as many seams in the columns—only 6 seams to align when sewing columns together. With this in mind, I assembled the quilt into 16 columns and then sewed those together.

Study Hall

A binary system is a system in which information can be reduced to one of two states, such as true/false, yes/no, on/off, 1/0. Most commonly, binary code is used for electronic data storage and logic processing, as well as cryptography and even Braille. It's a system of converting all data—words, numbers, symbols, images—into a series of 1s and 0s (yeses or nos). For this quilt, the alphabet is based on the ASCII system that is specific to computer programming.

Materials

Warm colors: 72 rectangles 3″ × 8″

Cool colors: 66 rectangles 3″ × 8″

Binding: ⅝ yard

Backing: 2¾ yards

Batting: 44″ × 57″

Cut It!

WOF = width of fabric

BINDING

- 6 strips 2½″ × WOF.

BACKING

- 2 strips 44″ × WOF: Subcut into 2 rectangles 24½″ × 44″.

Make It!

Assembling the Quilt Top

1. Lay out your rectangles according to the diagram. Remember to step back and take a picture to evaluate the fabric placement. Feel free to change pieces around as long as you switch warm colors only with other warm colors and cool colors only with other cool colors. Take a picture of the final layout. **Figure A**

2. Starting in the upper left corner, stack the pieces from the left column in order. Label the column. Repeat for the other 15 columns.

3. Starting with column 1, sew together pairs of rectangles. When you have 3 pairs, sew 2 pairs together, and sew 1 pair and the single rectangle together, so that you end up with 2 sections. Make sure that you keep track of the order of the blocks! Sew together the 2 sections.

4. Repeat Step 3 for the other 15 columns.

5. Press the seams of each column in one direction, alternating the direction from column to column; or press all seams open.

6. Lay out the quilt to make sure everything is still in the right place.

7. Sew the columns together in pairs. Make sure to nest the seams so that they line up properly. Continue sewing pairs together to form the quilt top. Press the seams open.

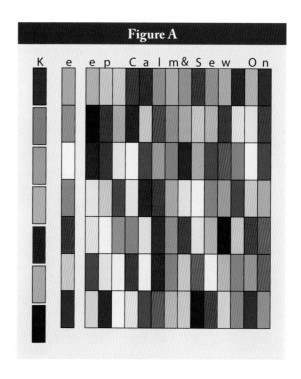

Figure A

K e e p C a l m& S e w O n

tip

As I sew, I stick a pin in the upper rectangle of each pair so that when I go back I don't have to worry about the pair being flipped over. When I sew a pair together, I leave the pin in the upper rectangle and remove it from the piece that is no longer a top block. Systems like this take some getting used to but will help you keep your pieces in order when you are chain piecing.

Assembling the Quilt Back

1. Arrange the remaining rectangles in rainbow order.

2. Take every other piece in the warm tones and lay them end to end, so that you have a row that is 7 blocks wide.

3. Create a second row using the 6 remaining warm blocks. Cut your 2 end pieces from the second row in half. Using only the halves on each end will offset the second row.

4. Repeat Steps 2 and 3 with the cool tones.

5. When your pieces are laid out in a way you like, sew the pieces together as you did for the top. Press.

6. Sew the 4 rows together. Press.

7. Sew the pieced rows to the 24½″ × 44″ backing pieces. Press.

> *Refer to pages 24–26 for information on sandwiching, quilting, and binding or go to tinyurl.com/quiltmaking-basics.*

Back of quilt

Fractal

------- Finished quilt size: 60˝ × 60˝ • Finished block sizes: 1¼˝, 2½˝, 5˝, 10˝, 20˝ -------

Inspiration

I don't remember seeing my first fractal, although I would guess it was at a laser show in the local planetarium when I was in high school. I think that math teachers love them because they are art that has mathematical significance and logic, so they are an easy way to bring creativity into a rigid subject.

You can see one of the most common fractals, the Sierpinski triangle, in my process sketches. It is made using equilateral or isosceles triangles, each smaller section building into a larger block that builds into an even larger block. It also looks like a more complex Triforce from *The Legend of Zelda*. I opted for a more original design using squares or rectangles and had a brainstorming session with my husband, who ultimately came up with the best design.

You'll notice that as you are piecing the quilt, many of the directions are repeated but with different color combinations. Because fractals repeat as you zoom in, the piecing remains the same, just on a smaller scale.

Planning

After drawing the design on graph paper, I noticed that the large corner squares created a visual line that I used to divide the quilt into thirds. I used the lines between the colors to help break up the quilt into even smaller sections, looking for color blocks and rows. You'll notice that as you piece this you are sewing Four-Patch blocks together to ultimately create a large Nine-Patch (each row is created by sewing together three blocks).

To add interest, I also decided to work each color in patchwork, although I have made this quilt with just solids and love the simplicity and how quickly it comes together. The blocks in each color get progressively smaller, working in halves to make piecing easier. For example, a Four-Patch of navy is the same size as one peach square.

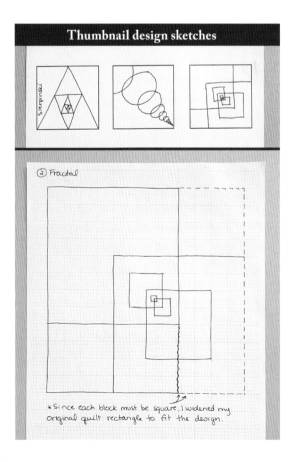

Thumbnail design sketches

Sierpinski

② Fractal

* Since each block must be square, I widened my original quilt rectangle to fit the design.

Skills

This is a great way to practice your precision in lining up seams and working with small blocks. I pressed all seams open on this quilt because I wanted the blocks to flow together and because the pressing diagram would have been crazy. If you press open you don't have to worry about accidentally pressing to the wrong side or, if your colors are different from mine, pressing to the light side.

tip

The tiny ⅝″ finished orange squares are actually cut larger and trimmed down. When working with small pieces (or large pieces!), don't be afraid to give yourself wiggle room for trimming at the end. You'll end up with more precise pieces, and the waste should be minimal.

Study Hall

A fractal is a system that displays *self-similarity* or *symmetry of scale*. No matter how far you zoom in or out of the pattern, it always looks the same. Many natural phenomena exhibit fractal geometry. Drainage patterns, coastlines, and clouds are examples of large fractal geometry. Small puddles are often the same shapes as large lakes.

Fractals are popularly used artistically, but they have mathematical value as well. Fractals are used in several technical fields, including data compression, biology, and fluid dynamics.

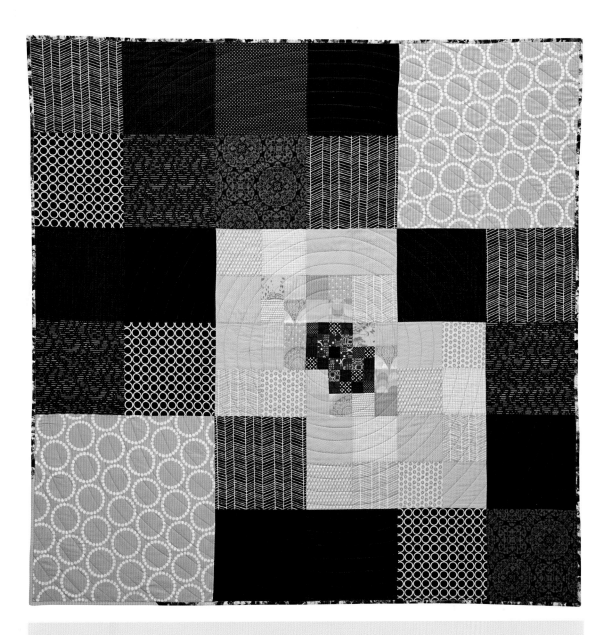

Materials

Orange: 24 squares of various prints 1¼″ × 1¼″

Gray: 21 squares of various prints 1¾″ × 1¾″

Green: 21 squares of various prints 3″ × 3″

Aqua: 21 squares of various prints 5½″ × 5½″

Navy: 21 squares of various prints 10½″ × 10½″

Peach: 2 squares 20½″ × 20½″

Black: 1 square 1¾″ × 1¾″

Binding: ¾ yard

Backing, gray: 2 yards

Backing, aqua: 2 yards

Backing accent: ¾ yard

Batting: 64″ × 64″

Cut It!

WOF = width of fabric

BACKING GRAY

- 1 piece 56″ × WOF: Trim off selvages. Subcut into 1 rectangle 12½″ × 56″, 1 rectangle 8½″ × 56″, 1 rectangle 6½″ × 56″, 1 rectangle 4½″ × 56″, and 1 rectangle 2½″ × 56″.

BACKING AQUA

- 1 piece 56″ × WOF: Trim off selvages. Subcut into 1 rectangle 12½″ × 56″, 1 rectangle 8½″ × 56″, 1 rectangle 6½″ × 56″, 1 rectangle 4½″ × 56″, and 1 rectangle 2½″ × 56″.

BACKING ACCENT

- 2 strips 9½″ × WOF: Trim off selvages.

BINDING

- 7 strips 2½″ × WOF.

Make It!

Assembling the Quilt Top

Press all seams open.

1. Sew together 24 orange squares into 12 pairs.

2. Sew together 2 pairs to create a Four-Patch block. Trim to 1¾″ × 1¾″. Make 6. Set aside.

3. Sew together 18 gray squares into 9 pairs.

4. Sew together 2 pairs to create a Four-Patch block. Make 3. Set aside remaining pairs and squares.

5. Repeat Steps 3 and 4 with the green, aqua, and navy squares. You should have 3 Four-Patch blocks, 3 pairs, and 3 squares of each color.

6. Following the center block and quilt assembly diagrams, sew together the Four-Patch blocks, the pairs, and squares as shown. **Figures A & B**

7. Sew together the blocks into rows. Join the rows.

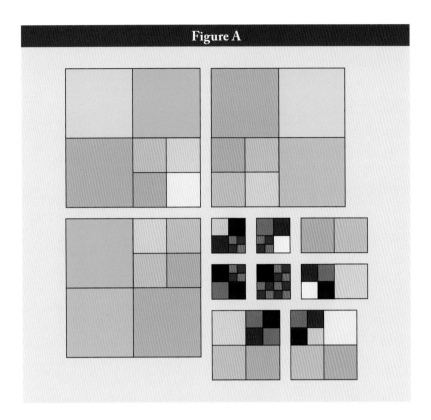

Figure A

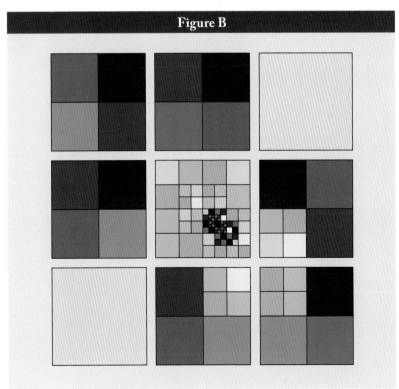

Figure B

Assembling the Quilt Back

1. Sew the gray 12½″ strip to the aqua 2½″ strip along the 56″ side. Repeat with the aqua 12½″ strip and the gray 2½″ strip. Press.

2. Sew the gray 8½″ strip to the aqua 4½″ strip. Repeat with the aqua 8½″ strip and the gray 4½″ strip. Press.

3. Sew the gray and aqua 6½″ strips together. Press.

4. Join the pieces from the previous steps as shown in the diagram. Press. **Figure C**

5. Measure 20″ from one side of the pieced strips and cut perpendicular to the strips. **Figure C**

6. Join the 9½″ strips of accent fabric along the 9½″ edges to make one long strip. Press.

7. Sew the accent fabric to the 20″ strip segment, aligning the tops of the fabric. Press. Trim the excess accent fabric.

8. Sew the 36″ strip segment to the other side of the accent fabric, making sure that the strips align. Press.

Refer to pages 24–26 for information on sandwiching, quilting, and binding or go to tinyurl.com/quiltmaking-basics.

Back of quilt

Figure C

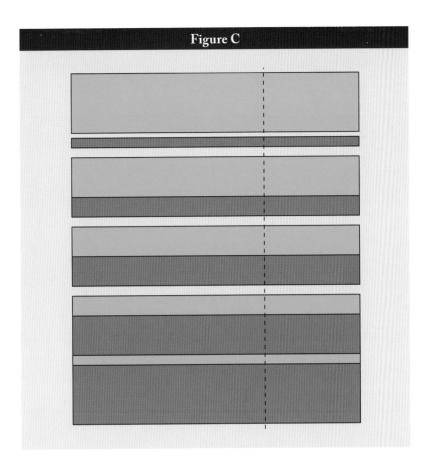

Quilting design

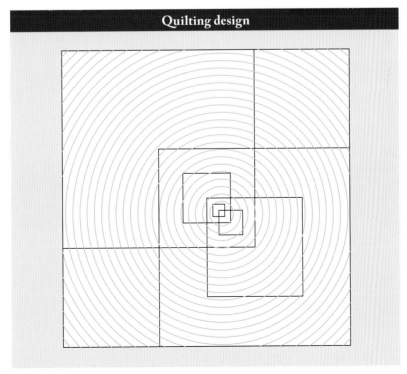

Scattered

Finished quilt size: 66″ × 51″ • Finished block size: 15″ × 15″

Inspiration

One of the first quilts I made had random pink blocks pieced into a brown background. I really liked the randomness and have wanted to make another, but it was at the bottom of a long list. While I was teaching graphing to my last group of students, I was reminded about this scatter quilt. In math we use scatter plots to graph points of data that don't have a pattern. This quilt shows the relationship between age and number of years sewing. Since we all start at different ages—some of us young and others later in life—the points are scattered and don't fall in a regular pattern. The quilting is the "line of best fit," a diagonal line showing that as age increases, so does number of years sewing.

Planning

After I had decided on the design and approximate dimensions, I looked at my data and estimated where the points would be. In class I'm precise; on quilts I tweak things to look right. There are many ways to piece points randomly, but these have a little more order. I decided to give myself a grid and move the points around until they lay fully in one block. From there it was a matter of looking for columns and rows within each block. Some are more complex than others because of where the points are.

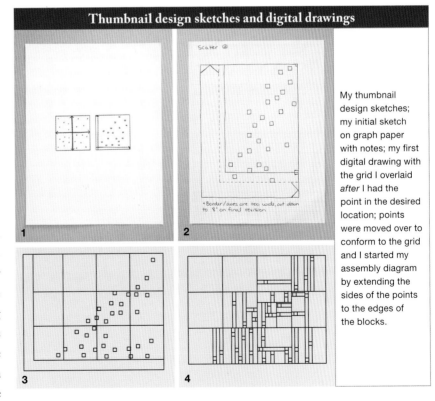

Thumbnail design sketches and digital drawings

My thumbnail design sketches; my initial sketch on graph paper with notes; my first digital drawing with the grid I overlaid *after* I had the point in the desired location; points were moved over to conform to the grid and I started my assembly diagram by extending the sides of the points to the edges of the blocks.

Skills

This quilt will challenge your logistic skills; this is a very organized way to create seemingly unorganized pieces. With so many differently sized pieces, it can be hard to keep track of them without a system. I've given some large cuts to make for the brown fabric and then broken down the cuts by block. Because the pieces vary in size so much (and can be similar in size), I found it easier to have the pieces laid out by block to make assembly quicker and easier. As I cut the pieces by block, I placed them in a pile and labeled the pile with a small piece of numbered tape. You also could label each piece with a letter.

Study Hall

Scatter plots are a way of representing two-variable data on a Cartesian coordinate plane. The variable plotted on the x-axis (horizontal axis) is controlled, such as time or age. The variable plotted on the y-axis (vertical axis) is what is being tested or observed, such as temperature or speed. After the data are recorded, scatter plots are used to look for patterns and to find correlations among the variables. The trend line, or line of best fit, is centered along the points of data so that an approximate slope can be used to better explain the positive or negative correlation. Scatter plots are an excellent example of how visual representations can relate information more easily than words or lists of numbers.

Materials

Brown: 3½ yards

Pinks and purples:
35 squares 2″ × 2″ and
4 squares 3¾″ × 3¾″;
distribute colors as desired

Cream: ¾ yard

Backing: 3¼ yards

Binding: ¾ yard

Batting: 70″ × 55″

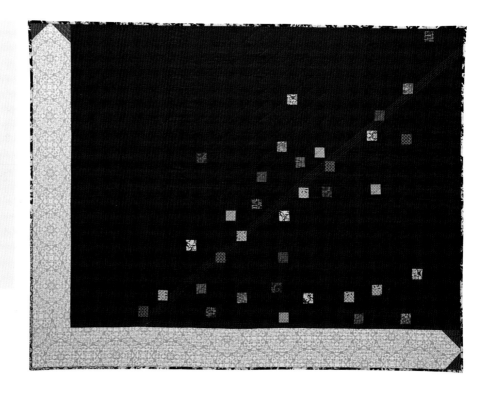

Cut It!

WOF = width of fabric

Cut the following strips; then subcut the pieces for the blocks from the strips.

BROWN

- 2 strips 15½″ × WOF
- 3 strips 16″ × WOF
- 7 strips 2″ × WOF
- 1 strip 7″ × WOF
- 1 strip 5″ × WOF

CREAM

- 3 strips 6½″ × WOF: Trim off selvages.

BINDING

- 7 strips 2½″ × WOF

Block 1

- 1 square 15½″ × 15½″

Block 2

- 1 square 15½″ × 15½″

Block 3

6 pieces

- 1 rectangle 16″ × 11½″ (*a*)
- 1 rectangle 2″ × 13″ (*b*)
- 1 square 2″ × 2″ (*c*)
- 1 rectangle 2″ × 16″ (*d*)
- 1 rectangle 2″ × 10½″ (*e*)
- 1 rectangle 2″ × 4½″ (*f*)

Block 4

1 square 15½″ × 15½″

Block 5

12 pieces

- 1 rectangle 16″ × 5¼″ (*a*)
- 1 rectangle 16″ × 3½″ (*d*)
- 1 rectangle 7¾″ × 5¼″ (*g*)
- 1 rectangle 7¼″ × 3″ (*i*)
- 1 rectangle 2¾″ × 3″ (*j*)
- 1 rectangle 2¾″ × 3¼″ (*l*)
- 1 rectangle 2″ × 5″ (*b*)
- 1 rectangle 2″ × 10″ (*c*)
- 1 rectangle 2″ × 13½″ (*e*)
- 1 rectangle 2″ × 1½″ (*f*)
- 1 rectangle 2″ × 3¾″ (*h*)
- 1 rectangle 2″ × 1¼″ (*k*)

Block 6

14 pieces

- 1 rectangle 16″ × 4½″ (*a*)
- 1 rectangle 16″ × 2¼″ (*j*)
- 1 rectangle 16″ × 2¾″ (*n*)
- 1 rectangle 2″ × 3″ (*b*)
- 1 rectangle 2″ × 12″ (*c*)
- 1 rectangle 2″ × 9½″ (*d*)
- 1 rectangle 2″ × 5½″ (*e*)
- 1 rectangle 2″ × 13″ (*f*)
- 1 square 2″ × 2″ (*g*)
- 1 rectangle 2″ × 4½″ (*h*)
- 1 rectangle 2″ × 10½″ (*i*)
- 1 rectangle 2″ × 1½″ (*k*)
- 1 rectangle 2″ × 8¼″ (*l*)
- 1 rectangle 2″ × 4¼″ (*m*)

Block 7

4 pieces

- 1 rectangle 16″ × 11¼″ (*a*)
- 1 rectangle 16″ × 3¾″ (*d*)
- 1 rectangle 2″ × 3½″ (*b*)
- 1 rectangle 2″ × 11½″ (*c*)

Block 8

21 pieces

- 1 rectangle 7″ × 5½″ (*a*)
- 1 rectangle 7″ × 1″ (*p*)
- 1 rectangle 7″ × 2¾″ (*s*)
- 1 rectangle 7″ × 5¼″ (*u*)
- 1 rectangle 5″ × 5½″ (*c*)
- 1 rectangle 5″ × 1½″ (*j*)
- 1 rectangle 5″ × 3″ (*l*)
- 1 rectangle 5″ × 5½″ (*o*)
- 1 rectangle 3″ × 11″ (*g*)
- 1 rectangle 2″ × 4″ (*b*)
- 1 rectangle 2″ × 3½″ (*k*)
- 1 rectangle 2″ × 1¾″ (*d*)
- 1 rectangle 2″ × 2¾″ (*e*)
- 2 rectangles 2″ × 5½″ (*f*) and (*t*)
- 1 rectangle 2″ × 5″ (*r*)
- 1 rectangle 2″ × 8½″ (*h*)
- 1 rectangle 2″ × 1½″ (*i*)
- 1 square 2″ × 2″ (*m*)
- 1 rectangle 2″ × 2½″ (*n*)
- 1 rectangle 2″ × 1″ (*q*)

Block 9

16 pieces

- 1 rectangle 9¼″ × 2¾″ (*a*)
- 1 rectangle 9¼″ × 12¼″ (*d*)
- 1 rectangle 5¾″ × 3″ (*g*)
- 1 rectangle 5¾″ × 2¾″ (*j*)
- 1 rectangle 5¾″ × 5¼″ (*l*)
- 1 rectangle 2″ × 4¾″ (*b*)
- 1 rectangle 2″ × 4¼″ (*k*)
- 2 rectangles 2″ × 3½″ (*c*) and (*h*)
- 2 rectangles 2″ × 1¾″ (*e*) and (*m*)
- 2 rectangles 2″ × 1¼″ (*i*) and (*p*)
- 1 rectangle 2″ × 10¼″ (*f*)
- 1 rectangle 2″ × 4½″ (*n*)
- 1 rectangle 2″ × 5″ (*o*)

Block 10

10 pieces

- 1 rectangle 16″ × 2¼″ (*a*)
- 1 rectangle 16″ × 3¼″ (*d*)
- 1 rectangle 16″ × 1¾″ (*g*)
- 1 rectangle 16″ × 5¾″ (*j*)
- 1 rectangle 2″ × 13½″ (*b*)
- 1 rectangle 2″ × 1½″ (*c*)
- 1 rectangle 2″ × 9½″ (*e*)
- 1 rectangle 2″ × 5½″ (*f*)
- 1 rectangle 2″ × 1¾″ (*h*)
- 1 rectangle 2″ × 13¼″ (*i*)

Block 11

10 pieces

- 1 rectangle 16″ × 8¼″ (*j*)
- 1 rectangle 6¾″ × 1½″ (*a*)
- 1 rectangle 6¾″ × 7″ (*d*)
- 1 rectangle 6¾″ × 5½″ (*g*)
- 1 rectangle 2″ × 1½″ (*b*)
- 1 rectangle 2″ × 4¼″ (*c*)
- 2 rectangles 2″ × 1¾″ (*e*) and (*h*)
- 1 rectangle 2″ × 4″ (*f*)
- 1 rectangle 2″ × 13¼″ (*i*)

Block 12

9 pieces

- 1 rectangle 16″ × 2¼″ (*a*)
- 1 rectangle 16″ × 3½″ (*d*)
- 1 rectangle 16″ × 6¾″ (*i*)
- 1 rectangle 2″ × 9½″ (*b*)
- 1 rectangle 2″ × 5½″ (*c*)
- 1 rectangle 2″ × 13¾″ (*e*)
- 1 rectangle 2″ × 1¼″ (*f*)
- 1 rectangle 2″ × 7″ (*g*)
- 1 rectangle 2″ × 8″ (*h*)

Make It!

Quilt Top

For all blocks, sew the pink and purple 2˝ squares to the corresponding pieces to make rows. Press all seams open. The unfinished blocks will measure 16˝ × 16˝ and will be trimmed to 15½˝ × 15½˝ for a 15˝ × 15˝ finished block.

Blocks 3, 6, 7, 10, and 12

Figure A

1. Sew the rows for the blocks together in pairs. Join the rows to make the blocks.

Block 5

Figure A

2. Sew together rows *a*, *b/c*, *d*, and *e/f*.

3. Sew together pieces *j*, *k*, and *l*; then sew to piece *i*.

4. Sew section *i/j/k/l* to pieces *g* and *h*. Sew to the section from Step 2.

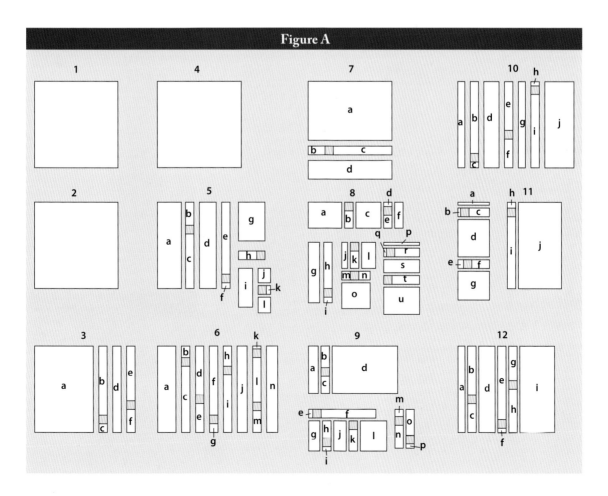

Figure A

Block 8
Figure B

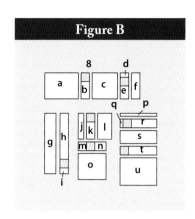

Figure B

5. Sew together pieces *a*, *b*, *c*, *d/e*, and *f* to create the top section.

6. Sew together pieces *g* and *h/i*.

7. Sew together pieces *j*, *k*, and *l*. Sew to piece *m/n* and then to piece *o*.

8. Sew together pieces *q/r* and *t*. Sew to pieces *p*, *s*, and *u*.

9. Sew together the sections.

Block 9
Figure C

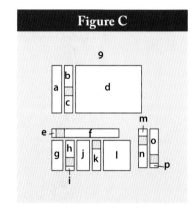

Figure C

10. Sew together pieces *a*, *b/c*, and *d* to create the top section.

11. Sew together pieces *g*, *h/i*, *j*, *k*, and *l*. Sew to piece *e/f*.

12. Sew together pieces *m/n* and *o/p*.

13. Sew together the sections.

Block 11
Figure D

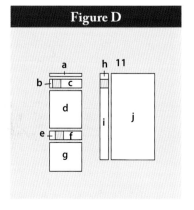

Figure D

14. Sew together pieces *b/c* and *e/f*. Sew to pieces *a*, *d*, and *g*.

15. Sew together rows *h/i* and *j*.

16. Sew together the sections.

Finishing the Quilt Top

1. Trim the blocks to 15½″ × 15½″.

2. Sew the blocks together in columns: 1/2/3, 4/5/6, 7/8/9, 10/11/12. Join the columns. Press all seams open.

3. Sew the 3 strips of cream fabric together, end to end. Press all seams open. Cut into 1 rectangle 6½″ × 45½″ and 1 rectangle 6½″ × 66½″.

4. Mark a diagonal line on the wrong side of the 3¾″ pink or purple squares. Lay a square on one end of the cream fabric, right sides together, aligning the corners. Sew on the diagonal line, trim, and press. Align a second square on the other corner so that it overlaps the seam you just sewed. Sew on the diagonal line, trim, and press. Repeat with the other 2 squares on the other cream piece.

5. Sew the cream 6½″ × 45½″ strip to the right edge of the quilt top. Press.

6. Sew the cream 6½″ × 66½″ strip to the bottom edge of the quilt top. Press.

> *Refer to pages 24–26 for information on sandwiching, quilting, and binding or go to tinyurl.com/quiltmaking-basics.*

Quilting design

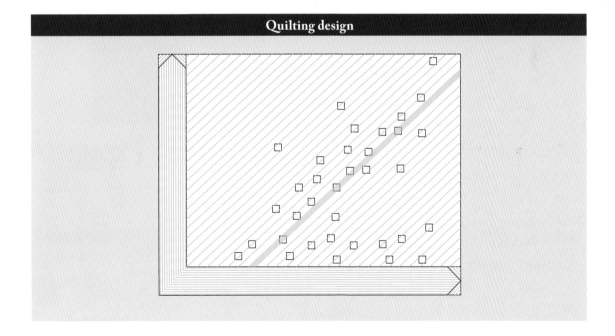

Angles

Sewing pieces together at angles can be tricky because you have to offset the pieces a bit to get them to line up correctly. Through the quilts in this chapter we'll look at different ways to sew angled pieces together and some fun designs that they can create.

States of Matter starts us off with triangles set into squares. These are pieced like Flying Geese and arranged in a few different ways to mimic the phases of matter—solid, liquid, and gas. *Calculus* takes you through piecing triangles with different angles and shows how triangles can forms arcs. Finally, with *Molecule* we take triangles and make them into hexagons and pentagons.

Piecing Angles

Into Rows

Excluding equilateral triangles, when you sew angled pieces—such as triangles and diamonds—into rows, you will have to offset the pieces. You want the needle to start and end in the angle created by the points of the two overlapping pieces.

When I'm working with triangles set into blocks—like Flying Geese or the blocks from *States of Matter*—I cut the background fabric larger and trim. Because the background fabric is cut larger, you do not need to worry about offsetting the pieces. **Figure A**

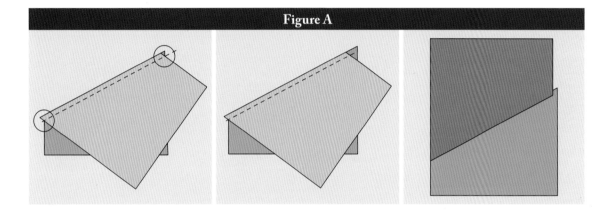

Figure A

Into Rounds

When sewing angled pieces into a "round" shape, like a hexagon, pentagon, or octagon, no offsetting is necessary. You just align the two pieces (which should have the same side length) and sew from the *tip outward*. **Figure B**

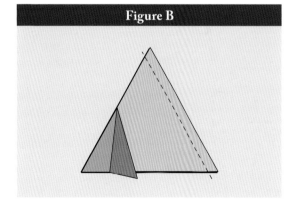

Figure B

States of Matter

---- Finished quilt size: 56″ × 63″ • Finished block size: 7″ × 7″ ----

Inspiration

I have a shirt that says, "Solid, Liquid, Gas. They all matter." The states of matter are something that we learn at a young age and interact with everyday. I started off with circles—and this quilt would look great with circles!—but I decided to go with triangles because they are easier to manipulate. You can have one block and turn it in four directions to get a different look.

Planning

To make just one block type and be able to turn it in different directions, the block had to be square, which meant that the base of the triangle had to be the same as the height. I drew and calculated and decided that it was just not going to be a common triangle! The angles are 53⅓°, 63⅓°, and 63⅓°. Not common. If you think you'll be using this kind of triangle in more than one project, invest in a custom template.

I like generous lap quilts, so I started with a 55″ × 65″ box and looked for numbers that have multiples close to both of those numbers. I wanted 9 rows, 3 for each state. I then divided 65 by 9. The result was, of course, not a whole number (but at least it was rational!), so I rounded down to 7 and decided on 7″ × 7″ finished blocks.

Thumbnail design sketch

Skills

This quilt is great for practice marking your ruler or cutting mat. You will be cutting so many pieces using the same angle that it's easier to use the marked mat than to follow a paper template for each cut. This is also a time to practice patience. I like perfect blocks, which means I make them larger and trim them down. Trimming down 81 blocks takes patience, but the end result is worth it.

Study Hall

The state or phase of matter depends on the activity and arrangement of the molecules that make up the matter. In a solid state such as ice, the molecules are packed closely together and the forces between them are strong enough that they can't move in relation to each other, although they do vibrate. Solids have a definite shape and volume. When a solid is heated above its melting point, it becomes a liquid. Liquids still have a constant volume, but the molecules have enough energy to slide past each other. A liquid will conform to the shape of its container. In a gas, the individual molecules have enough kinetic energy (such as added heat) that they have little or no interaction with each other. Gases (such as steam) will take on the shape and volume of the container.

Materials

Turquoise: 3 yards

Dark gray: 6 fat quarters of various prints

Medium gray: 6 fat quarters of various prints

Light gray: 4 fat quarters of various prints

Gray solid for backing: 3¼ yards

Binding: ¾ yard

Batting: 60″ × 67″

Patterns

Cut It!

WOF = width of fabric

TURQUOISE

- 9 strips 7¾″ × WOF: Subcut into 132 wedges using pattern *b*. If using a print, cut with the fabric folded to yield 66 mirror-image pairs.

- 3 strips 7½″ × WOF: Subcut into 15 squares 7½″ × 7½″ and 2 rectangles 7½″ × 2½″.

DARK GRAY

From each fat quarter, cut

- 2 strips 7½″ × 20″: Subcut into 5 triangles using pattern *a* (27 triangles total required).

MEDIUM GRAY

From each fat quarter, cut

- 2 strips 7½″ × 20″: Subcut into 5 triangles using pattern *a* (27 triangles total required).

LIGHT GRAY

From each fat quarter, cut

- 1 strip 7½″ × 20″: Subcut into 3 triangles using pattern *a* (12 triangles total required).

GRAY BACKING

- 2 strips 34″ × WOF: Subcut into 2 rectangles 34″ × 38″.

- 2 strips 16″ × WOF: Subcut into 2 rectangles 16″ × 34″.

BINDING

- 7 strips 2½″ × WOF.

Make It!

Refer to Into Rows on page 67 for more information about piecing the angles.

1. Sew a turquoise wedge to the right side of each of the gray triangles. Press seams.

2. Sew a turquoise wedge to the left side of each triangle. Press seams.

3. Trim blocks to 7½˝ × 7½˝.

4. Set aside 3 blocks of each shade for the quilt back. Arrange the remaining blocks according to the diagram. Use dark gray blocks on the bottom 3 rows, medium gray blocks in the middle, and light gray blocks on the top 3 rows. Use the 7½˝ × 7½˝ squares to fill in the blank spaces in the top 3 rows.

5. Making sure to mark the order of the blocks and the rows (take a quick picture), sew together the blocks in each row. Sew together the pieces into pairs and then sew the pairs together until the row is complete. Press.

6. Sew together the rows, making sure to align seams. Press all seams with steam. **Figure A**

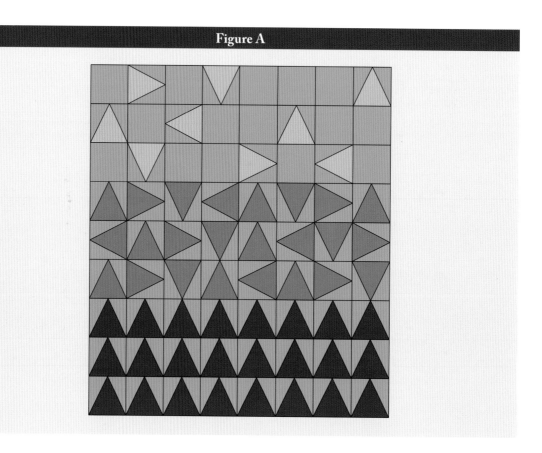

Figure A

Assembling the Quilt Back

1. For the quilt back, arrange the 9 triangle blocks from darkest to lightest, creating a column. Place a 7½˝ × 2½˝ turquoise rectangle at the top and bottom of the column.

2. Sew the blocks into pairs; then join the pairs to the remaining block and turquoise rectangles.

3. Sew the 16˝ × 34˝ gray backing rectangles together on the 16˝ edges to make a 16˝ × 67½˝ piece. Repeat with the 34˝ × 38˝ rectangles, creating a 38˝ × 67½˝ piece. Press seams open.

4. Center the dark gray pieces on either side of the triangle column and join the pieces. Press.

Refer to pages 24–26 for information on sandwiching, quilting, and binding or go to tinyurl.com/quiltmaking-basics.

Quilting design

Back of quilt

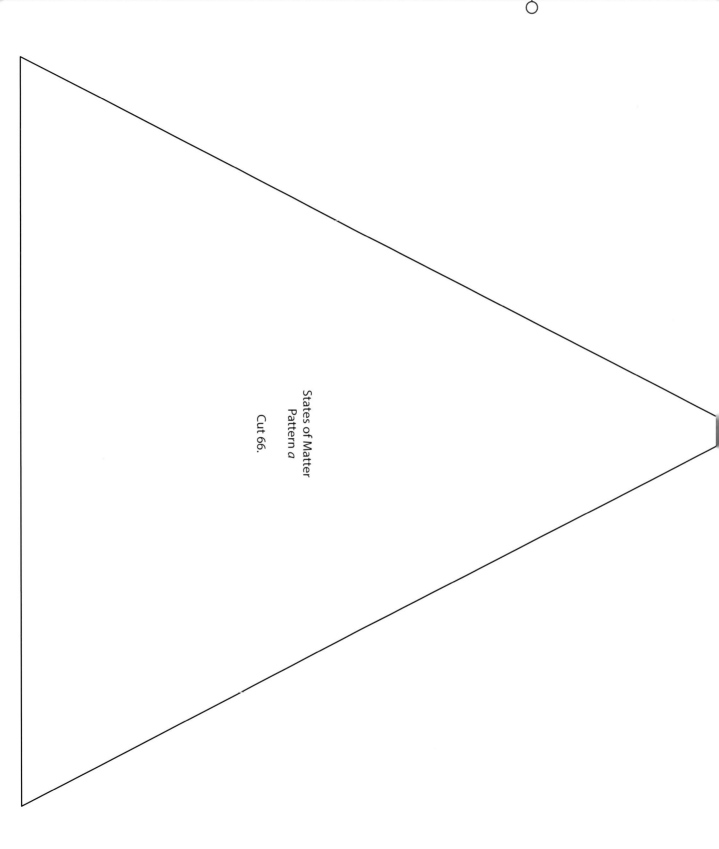

States of Matter
Pattern *a*

Cut 66.

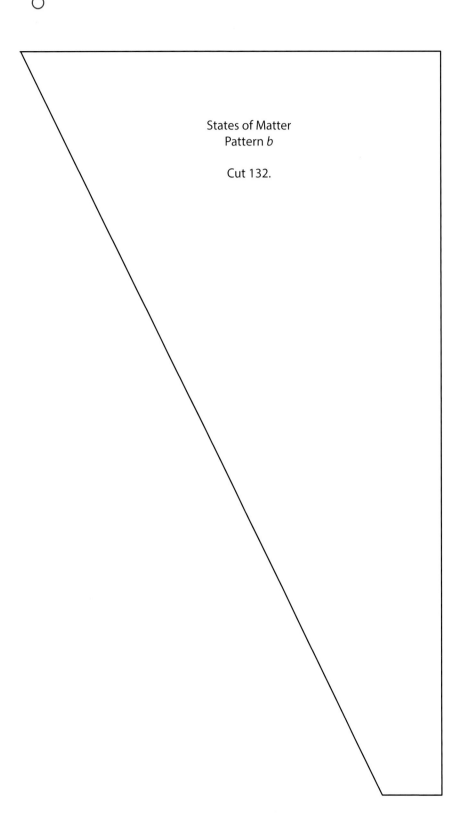

States of Matter
Pattern *b*

Cut 132.

Calculus

Inspiration

I knew that I wanted to show how progressively more triangles can create curves. I thought about sine and cosine curves, and wave amplitude and wavelength. Finally I settled on showing how calculus works. Sometimes I go through pages of diagrams to get to a design I like, and other times the design is just there. Although it took me a while to decide how to blend curves with triangles, once I had settled on calculus, the design just came to me.

Planning

Knowing that I wanted to show how progressively more pieces per block creates a round shape, I started by designing blocks rather than with set dimensions in mind. One triangle per block is a half-square triangle (HST), and I wanted to include a technique for making these. Then I divided the block into two equal pieces, then three, then four. Only after I had designed the blocks did I decide how big each block would be (5″ finished) and worked the dimensions of the quilt around that block size.

When you are working with pieces that require templates, first draw the block to the full size on graph paper, not including seam allowances. Make as many copies as there are pieces. For example, if there are four unique pieces, you will need four copies. Cut each template from a separate copy, making sure to use your quilting ruler to add ¼″ on each side. Label the templates.

Thumbnail design sketches

Skills

This quilt actually comes together quite quickly once you get into the groove. On this quilt you'll have to piece the triangles two different ways. When you join the brown background pieces to the triangles, you will have to offset the pieces, as you would when sewing angles in a line (see page 67). After adding a brown background piece to each triangle, start to assemble the triangles into 5½″ blocks. At this point you'll piece the angled sides as you would to make a round shape, lining up the sides and sewing from tip to background. Piecing into blocks and then sewing the blocks together is a great way to get the points to line up in the center. I suggest pressing all seams open to reduce bulk at the center.

Study Hall Calculus, or more specifically integral calculus, is the field of study concerned with finding the area under a curve. This is accomplished by breaking down complex shapes, like curves, into simple shapes, like triangles and rectangles, and then reducing the size of the simple shapes further and further. The smaller the simple shape is, the more accurate the area of the curve is.

This quilt has 4 different types of triangles in it. The orange triangles are HSTs. Four of these make a square, not a curve at all! The coral triangles are 45° at the point; thus 2 together make a 90° or right angle. Eight of these together make an octagon block. You can see that by cutting the 90° HST in half, the curve is starting to appear. The red triangles measure 30°, and there are 3 per block. Shapes with 12 wedges or sides are called dodecagons. The blue triangles measure 22.5°. Two together would make a 45° angle and 4 wedges will make a right angle. Because there are 16 pieces in the rounded version of this shape, it's called a hexadecagon (or a hexakaidecagon—*hexa* meaning 6 + *deca* meaning 10 = 16!). The smaller the wedge angle is, the closer you get to a curve. What if I had 40 wedges per shape? From a distance you wouldn't be able to tell that it wasn't a circle!

Materials

Brown: 2¼ yards

Orange prints: 2 coordinating fat quarters

Orange solid: ½ yard

Coral print: fat quarter

Coral solids: ½ yard each of 2 coordinating solids

Red prints: 4 coordinating fat quarters

Red solid: ½ yard

Blue prints: 4 coordinating fat quarters

Blue solid (includes binding): 1 yard

Backing: 2¼ yards

Batting: 44″ × 59″

Patterns

Cut It!

WOF = width of fabric

BROWN

- 2 strips 8½″ × WOF: Subcut into 5 squares 8½″ × 8½″.

- 2 strips 5⅞″ × WOF: *With fabric folded*, subcut into 40 wedges using pattern *a2* (20 mirror-image pairs).

- 2 strips 3⅝″ × WOF: *With fabric folded*, subcut into 40 wedges using pattern *b2* (20 mirror-image pairs).

- 2 strips 3⅛″ × WOF: Subcut into 20 pieces using pattern *b3*.

- 1 strip 2¾″ × WOF: *With fabric folded*, subcut into 40 wedges using pattern *c2* (20 mirror-image pairs).

- 2 strips 3¾″ × WOF: *With fabric folded*, subcut into 40 wedges using pattern *c3* (20 mirror-image pairs).

- 5 strips 3½″ × WOF: Trim to 3½″ × 40½″.

ORANGE

From each of 2 print fat quarters, cut

- 1 strip 8½″ × 20″: Subcut into 1 square 8½″ × 8½″.

From the solid, cut

- 1 strip 8½″ × WOF: Subcut into 3 squares 8½″ × 8½″.

- 1 strip 5½″ × WOF: Trim to 5½″ × 20½″.

CORAL

From the print fat quarter, cut

- 2 strips 5⅛″ × 20″: Subcut into 12 of triangle *a1*.

From 1 solid, cut

- 1 strip 5⅛″ × WOF: Subcut into 12 of triangle *a1*.

From the other solid, cut

- 1 strip 5⅛″ × WOF: Subcut into 16 of triangle *a1*.

- 1 strip 5½″ × WOF: Trim to 5½″ × 20½″.

RED

From each of 4 print fat quarters, cut

- 1 strip 5⅜″ × 20″: Subcut into 11 of triangle *b1* (44 total).

From the solid, cut

- 1 strip 5⅜″ × WOF: Subcut into 18 of triangle *b1*.

- 1 strip 5½″ × WOF: Trim to 5½″ × 20½″.

BLUE

From each of 4 print fat quarters, cut

- 2 strips 5½″ × 20″: Subcut into 15 of triangle *c1* (60 total).

From the solid, cut

- 1 strip 5½″ × WOF: Subcut into 20 of triangle *c1*.

- 1 strip 5½″ × WOF: Trim to 5½″ × 20½″.

- 6 strips 2½″ × WOF for binding.

BACKING

- 2 strips 5½″ × WOF: Subcut into 4 squares 5½″ × 5½″ and 1 rectangle 5½″ × 30½″.

- 1 strip 9½″ × WOF: Trim to 9½″ × 30½″.

- 1 strip 44½″ × WOF: Subcut into 1 rectangle 44½″ × 22½″ and 1 rectangle 44½″ × 7½″.

Make It!

Orange Row

1. With right sides together, match each 8½˝ brown square with an orange square. Sew around all 4 sides and then cut twice diagonally. Press seams open and trim the half-square triangles to 5½˝ square.

2. Lay out the HST blocks according to the diagram, setting aside 4 blocks for the quilt back. Sew the blocks together into 2 rows and then sew the rows together. **Figure A**

3. Sew the remaining 4 blocks together as shown. **Figure B**

Coral Row

4. Sew the coral triangles (*a1*) to the brown wedges (*a2*). If you are using a solid that doesn't have a right side and a wrong side, make sure you mark half of the wedges as mirror-image pieces. Make 40 mirror-image wedges (20 in each direction).

5. Sew the pieces together in pairs of mirror-image wedges to make 20 blocks 5½˝ × 5½˝.

6. Lay out the blocks according to the diagram, setting aside 4 blocks for the quilt back. Sew the blocks together to create 2 rows and then sew the rows together. **Figure A**

7. Sew the remaining 4 blocks together as shown. **Figure B**

Red Row

8. Sew the red triangles (*b1*) to the brown wedges (*b2* and *b3*). If you are using a solid that doesn't have a right side and a wrong side, make sure you mark half of the *b2* wedges as mirror-image pieces. Make 40 mirror-image pieces with *b2* (20 in each direction) and 20 pieces with *b3*.

9. Sew the mirror-image *b2* blocks to either side of the *b3* piece.

10. Lay out the blocks according to the diagram, setting aside 4 blocks for the quilt back. Sew the blocks together to create 2 rows and then sew the rows together. **Figure A**

11. Sew the remaining 4 blocks together as shown. **Figure B**

Blue Row

12. Sew the blue triangles (*c1*) to the brown wedges (*c2* and *c3*). If you are using a solid that doesn't have a right side and a wrong side, make sure you mark half of the wedges as mirror-image pieces. Make 40 mirror-image wedges with *c2* (20 in each direction) and 40 mirror-image wedges with *c3* (20 in each direction).

13. Sew the mirror-image wedges together to make 20 blocks 5½˝ × 5½˝.

14. Lay out the blocks according to the diagram, setting aside 4 blocks for the quilt back. Sew the blocks together to create 2 rows and then sew the rows together. **Figure A**

15. Sew the remaining 4 blocks together as shown. **Figure B**

Assembling the Quilt Top

1. Sew a 3½˝ brown strip to the top of each of the color rows. Sew the remaining strip to the bottom of the blue row. Press.

2. Sew the rows together. Press. **Figure A**

Figure A

Assembling the Quilt Back

1. Sew together the blocks to create a 20½˝ square. **Figure B**

2. Sew the orange and blue 5½˝ × 20½˝ rectangles to either side of the square.

3. Sew the 5½˝ background squares to the ends of the red and coral 5½˝ × 20½˝ rectangles. Press. Then sew the strips to the top and bottom of the square.

4. Sew the 5½˝ × 30½˝ and 9½˝ × 30½˝ background rectangles to opposite sides of the square.

5. Sew the remaining background pieces to the top and bottom of the piece from Step 4. **Figure B**

Refer to pages 24–26 for information on sandwiching, quilting, and binding or go to tinyurl.com/quiltmaking-basics.

Back of quilt

Figure B

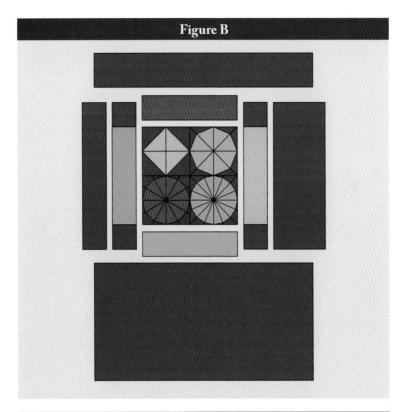

Quilting design

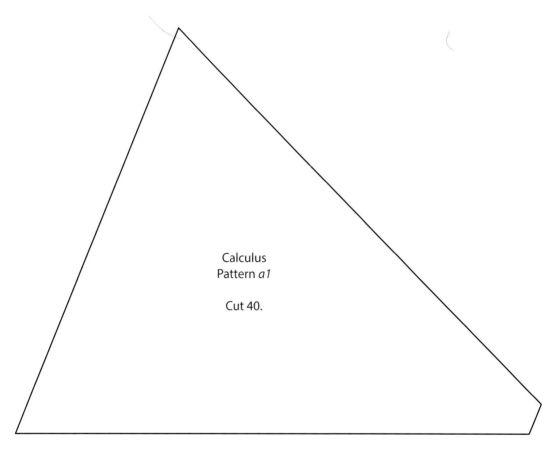

Calculus
Pattern *a1*

Cut 40.

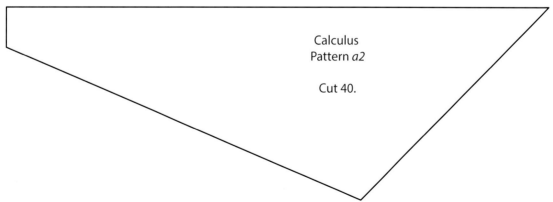

Calculus
Pattern *a2*

Cut 40.

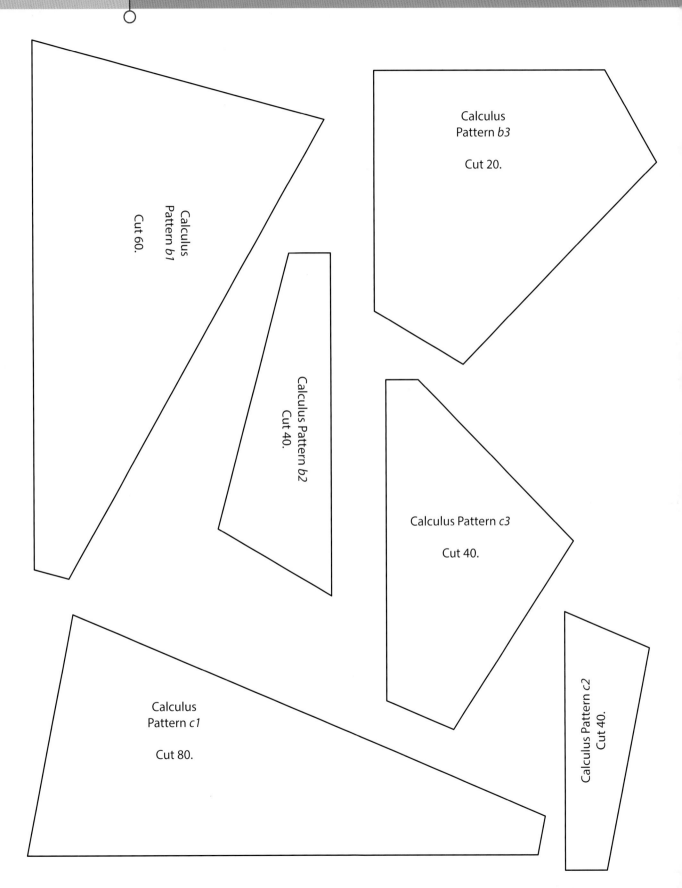

Calculus
Pattern *b1*

Cut 60.

Calculus
Pattern *b3*

Cut 20.

Calculus Pattern *b2*
Cut 40.

Calculus Pattern *c3*

Cut 40.

Calculus
Pattern *c1*

Cut 80.

Calculus Pattern *c2*
Cut 40.

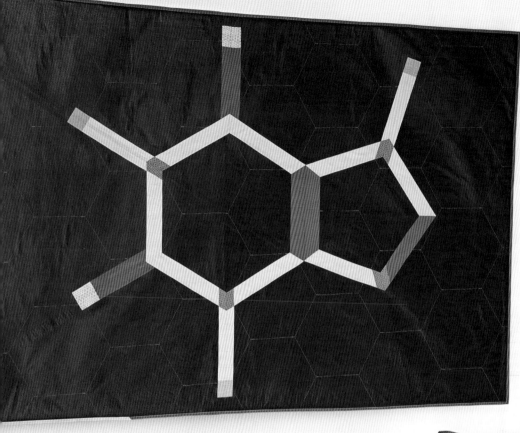

Molecular

-------------------- Finished quilt size: 50″ × 70″ --------------------

Inspiration

I remember first seeing molecule jewelry on Etsy years ago. I immediately bought a pair of earrings for my sister. Now we see molecules on everything—mugs, clothes, accessories, computer supplies—so why not a quilt? I looked at a few different molecules: caffeine, serotonin, dopamine, and DNA GCTA molecules. Caffeine seems to be the most known and common, although I'm a decaf girl myself.

Planning

This quilt was intense, and I used every single brain cell breaking this down! What first stood out to me was that the caffeine molecule is made of a hexagon and pentagon, two shapes that I'm familiar with. I've pieced hexagons in wedges before and knew that piecing pentagons would be similar. Next I thought about the different bonds and how to show those. Finally I looked at the elements and their placement. I knew that I would be using wedges, so I extended the lines to the edges of the quilt.

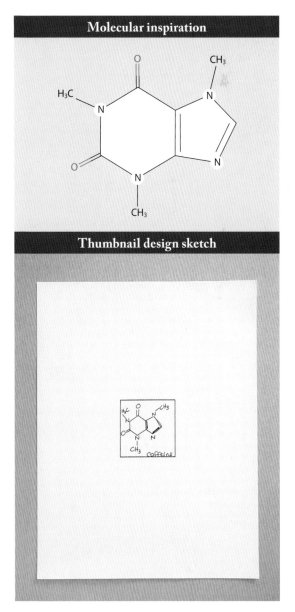

Molecular inspiration

Thumbnail design sketch

Skills

Although I tried to make this quilt as simple as possible to assemble, sometimes there's no getting around Y-seams. Because hexagons have six sides it's easy to split them in half; but pentagons have only five sides, so you'll always have to join the wedges with a Y-seam. Have no fear; it's not difficult! This quilt should make you an expert at using the 30° and 60° lines on a ruler and cutting mat. Again, that pentagon is going to cause some problems because its 72° and 54° angles aren't already marked. I'm including a slope chart (page 126) so that you can mark your ruler, or you can use a protractor (you know, that half circle that you probably haven't used since middle school).

Study Hall There are many different atoms and each one is a different element (they are organized into the periodic table of elements). Atoms can have a positive or negative charge (these are the charges I talked about memorizing in the Introduction), but they want to be neutral so they bond with atoms that have an opposite charge. Bonded together, these atoms make molecules. A molecule is the smallest particle of a substance that retains the properties of that substance; if you break it down any further, it will be something else.

Recently scientists have become more interested in the angles formed by the bonds between atoms. The angle of the bonds in water (H_2O) is what makes it so unique and why it bonds so easily to other molecules.

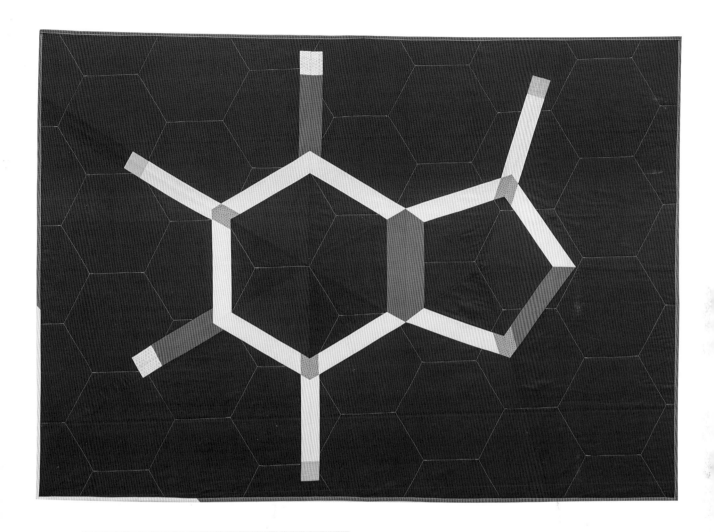

Materials

Navy: 3½ yards

Light pink: ½ yard

Hot pink: ¼ yard

Beige: fat quarter

Yellow: fat quarter

Green: fat quarter

Aqua: fat quarter

Binding: ¾ yard

Backing: 3½ yards

Batting: 54″ × 74″

Protractor

Cut It!

WOF = width of fabric

NAVY

- 1 strip 9¼″ × WOF: Subcut into 6 triangles 60° (piece *a*).

- 1 strip 7″ × WOF: Subcut into 5 triangles 72° (piece *b*).

- 1 strip 29½″ × WOF: Subcut into 2 rectangles 29½″ × 19″ (pieces *c* and *d*).

- 1 strip 20″ × WOF: Subcut into 2 rectangles 20″ × 10″ (pieces *g* and *i*) and 1 rectangle 20″ × 9¾″ (piece *h*).

- 1 strip 19½″ × WOF: Subcut into 1 rectangle 19½″ × 16″ (piece *j*) and 1 rectangle 19½″ × 17″ (piece *k*).

- 1 strip 25½″ × WOF: Subcut into 2 rectangles 25½″ × 19″ (pieces *l* and *m*).

- 2 strips 1½″ × WOF: Subcut into 2 rectangles 1½″ × 2½″, 2 rectangles 1½″ × 14″, and 2 rectangles 1½″ × 7″.

- 1 strip 1¾″ × WOF: Subcut into 2 rectangles 1¾″ × 2½″ and 2 rectangles 1¾″ × 14″.

LIGHT PINK

- 3 strips 2½″ × WOF: Subcut into 1 rectangle 2½″ × 13″ and 7 rectangles 2½″ × 12″.

- 2 strips 1½″ × WOF: Subcut into 6 rectangles 1½″ × 10″.

HOT PINK

- 1 strip 2½″ × WOF: Subcut into 2 rectangles 2½″ × 13″ and 1 rectangle 2½″ × 12″.

- 2 strips 1¾″ × WOF: Subcut into 4 rectangles 1¾″ × 10″.

BEIGE

- 1 strip 1¾″ × 20″: Subcut into 4 rectangles 1¾″ × 3″.

YELLOW

- 1 strip 1½″ × 20″: Subcut into 4 rectangles 1½″ × 2½″.

GREEN

- 1 strip 1½″ × 20″: Subcut into 2 rectangles 1½″ × 2½″.

AQUA

- 1 strip 2½″ × 20″: Fold in half and cut two 60° wedges 1½″ wide and two 54° wedges 1½″ wide (because the fabric is folded, this will result in 8 wedges).

BINDING

- 7 strips 2½″ × WOF.

BACKING

- 2 strips 56″ × WOF: Trim off selvages.

Figure A

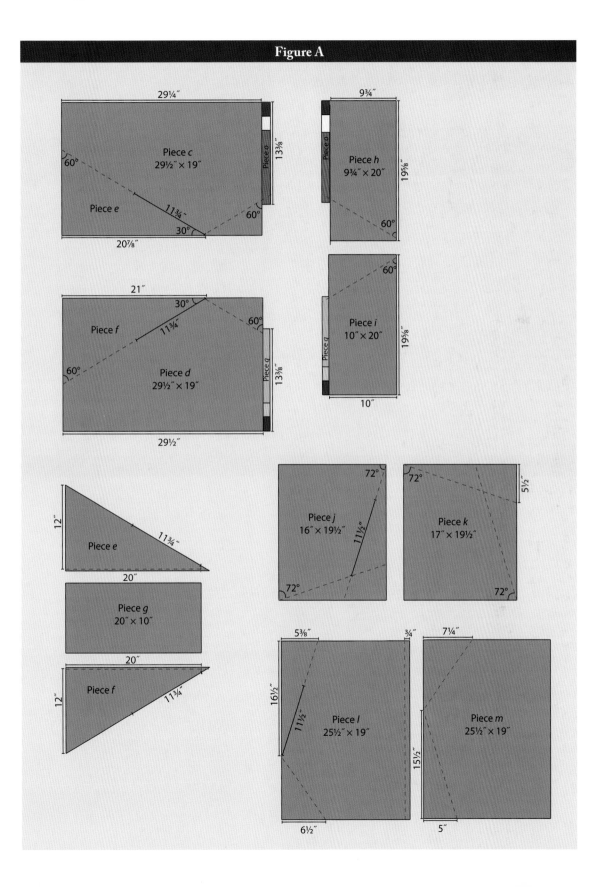

Make It!

Assembling the Outer Spokes

Refer to Figure B for the following steps.

1. Sew a navy 1¾″ × 2½″ rectangle to a beige rectangle. Then sew the beige side to a hot pink 1¾″ × 10″ rectangle. Press seams open. Set aside. Repeat with the other navy, beige, and hot pink rectangles of the same size (piece *o*).

2. Sew a navy 1¾″ × 14″ rectangle to a beige rectangle. Then sew the beige side to a hot pink 1¾″ × 10″ rectangle. Press seams open. Set aside. Repeat with the other navy, beige, and hot pink rectangles of the same size (piece *p*).

3. Sew a navy 1½″ × 2½″ rectangle to a yellow rectangle. Then sew the yellow side to a light pink 1½″ × 10″ rectangle. Press seams open. Set aside. Repeat with the other navy, yellow, and light pink rectangles of the same size (piece *q*).

4. Sew a navy 1½″ × 7″ rectangle to a yellow rectangle. Then sew the yellow side to a light pink 1½″ × 10″ rectangle. Press seams open. Set aside. Repeat with the other navy, yellow, and light pink rectangles of the same size (piece *r*).

5. Sew a navy 1½″ × 14″ rectangle to a green rectangle. Then sew the green side to a light pink 1½″ × 10″ rectangle. Press seams open. Set aside. Repeat with the other navy, green, and light pink rectangles of the same size (piece *s*).

Figure B

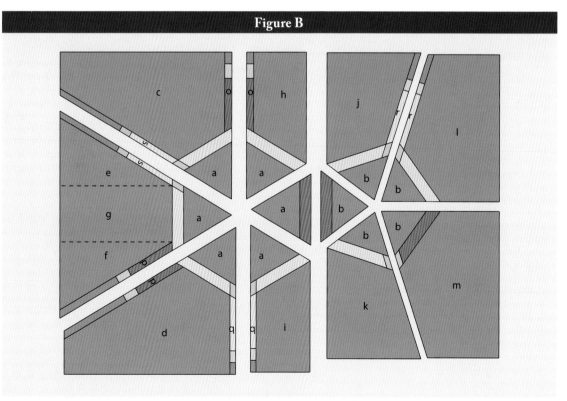

Piecing in the Nitrogen (Aqua)

1. Place 2 light pink 2½″ × 12″ rectangles *wrong sides* together. Cut off one side at a 60° angle, starting at a corner. *The angle inside the pink piece is 60°, and the angle of the piece that is cut off is 30°. Lay your ruler out first and check to make sure it looks correct before you cut.* Set aside. Repeat with 1 more pair of light pink rectangles.

2. Pair each of 4 aqua 60° wedges with its corresponding light pink piece; this will create 2 pairs. Place the aqua fabric right sides together on the pink, offsetting the tips ¼″. Sew and press.

3. Place 2 light pink 2½″ × 12″ rectangles *wrong sides* together. Cut off one end at a 54° angle. Set aside. Repeat with a light pink and hot pink pair.

4. Pair each of 4 aqua 54° wedges with its corresponding light pink piece; this will create 2 pairs. Place the aqua fabric right sides together on the pink, offsetting the angle ¼″. Sew and press.

Assembling the Hexagon Half

Refer to the quilt photo on page 89, the cutting diagrams on page 91, and the assembly diagram on page 92.

1. Sew the 60° light pink and aqua wedges to 4 of the 60° triangles along the straight-grain (nonbias) edge, offsetting the pieces so that the angle of the *aqua* will match the angle on the triangle. Press. Trim excess *pink* fabric.

2. Take a 60° triangle and the 2½″ × 13″ light pink strip. Center the light pink strip along the straight edge of the triangle. Sew and press. Trim excess pink fabric. Repeat with the remaining piece *a* triangle and the 2½″ × 13″ hot pink strip.

3. Sew 1 piece *o* to the left side of piece *h*, aligning the navy edges at the top. Press. Measure down 19⅝″ from the upper right corner. Cut off the bottom at a 60° angle. Sew piece *q* to the left side of piece *i*, aligning the navy edges at the bottom. Press. Measure up 19⅝″ from the lower right corner. Cut off the top at a 60° angle.

4. Sew piece *o/h* to the piece *a* triangle with a light pink edge. Press.

5. Sew piece *q/i* to the piece *a* triangle with a light pink edge and aqua on the end. The aqua should align with the pink and yellow strip. Press.

6. Place piece *c* with the right side facing up. Cut off ¼″ from the right edge. Measure over 20⅞″ from the lower left corner. Cut off the corner at a 30° angle to make piece *e*. Set aside.

7. Measure and mark 11¾″ from the 20⅞″ point along the angled side you just cut. Sew piece *s* to the cut edge, aligning the seam between the green and navy pieces at the mark. Press. Trim ends to match background.

8. Sew the remaining piece *o* along the 19″ side, aligning the navy ends at the top. Press.

9. Measure down 13⅜″ from the upper right corner. Cut off the corner with a 60° angle.

10. Sew a piece *a* triangle with aqua on the end along the edge you just cut. The aqua should align with the pink and green strip. Press.

11. Place piece *d* with the right side facing up. Measure over 21″ from the upper left corner. Cut off the corner at a 30° angle to make piece *f*. Set aside.

12. Measure and mark 11¾″ from the 21″ point along the angled side you just cut. Sew piece *p* to the cut edge, aligning the seam between the beige and navy pieces at the mark. Press. Trim ends to match background.

13. Sew the remaining piece *q* along the 19″ side, aligning the navy ends at the bottom. Press.

14. Measure up 13⅜″ from the bottom right corner. Cut off the corner with a 60° angle.

15. Sew a piece *a* triangle with aqua on the end along the edge you just cut. The aqua should align with the pink and yellow strip. Press.

16. Trim pieces *e* and *f* along the long straight edge so that the triangles are 12″ long. Trim off the tip so that the long side is 20″.

17. Measure 11¾″ from the cut-off tip along the hypotenuse. Mark.

18. Sew piece *s* to piece *e*, aligning the seam between the navy and green with the mark. Press. Trim.

19. Sew piece *p* to piece *f*, aligning the seam between the navy and beige with the mark. Press. Trim.

20. Sew pieces *e* and *f* to piece *g*. Press.

21. Sew a piece *a* triangle with aqua on the end to the short straight side. The aqua should align with the pink and green strip. Press.

22. Sew the upper left corner, piece *c*, to the middle wedge, piece *e/f/g*. Start at the tip and sew toward the outer edge. You do not need to offset the pieces; the seams between the aqua, pink, and green pieces should be aligned, as well as the tip and outer edge. Press.

23. Sew the lower left corner, piece *d*, to the other side of the middle wedge, piece *e/f/g*, again starting at the tip and sewing outward. Press. Set aside.

24. Sew piece *o/h* to triangle *a* with the hot pink strip. Start at the tip and sew toward the outer edge. You do not need to offset the pieces. Press.

25. Sew piece *q/i* to the other side of triangle *a*. Press.

26. Sew the left section from Step 23 to this middle section so that the tips of the triangles are aligned. Press. Set aside. This is the left half of the quilt.

Assembling the Pentagon Half

Refer to the quilt photo on page 89, the cutting diagrams on page 91, and the assembly diagram on page 92.

1. Sew the 54° light pink and aqua wedges to 4 of the 72° triangles (piece *b*) along the nonbias edge, offsetting the pieces so that the angle of the *aqua* will match the angle on the triangle. Press. Trim excess *pink* fabric.

2. Center the 2½″ × 13″ hot pink strip on the remaining 54° triangle. Sew and press. Trim excess pink fabric.

3. Trim piece *j* according to the diagram. Cut 72° wedges off the bottom and right sides, starting at the corners. Measure 11½″ from the new bottom right point. Mark.

4. Sew piece *r* to the right side, aligning the seam between yellow and navy with the mark. Press. Trim.

5. Sew a piece *b* triangle with light pink and aqua on the end to the bottom, aligning the pink with the aqua.

6. Trim piece *k* according to the diagram. Cut 72° wedges off the top and right sides, starting at the corners.

7. Sew a piece *b* triangle with light pink and aqua on the end to the top angle, aligning aqua with the edge of the block.

8. Trim piece *l* according to the diagram. Cut ¾″ off the right side. Cut the wedges off the upper and lower left corners. Measure 11½″ from the new point. Mark.

9. Sew piece *r* to the upper left side, aligning the seam between yellow and navy with the mark. Press. Trim.

10. Sew a piece *b* triangle with light pink and aqua on the end to the bottom left angled corner, aligning the pink with the aqua.

11. Trim piece *m* according to the diagram. Cut wedges off the upper and lower left corners.

12. Sew a piece *b* triangle with hot pink and aqua on the end to the top angled side, aligning aqua with the edge of the block.

13. Sew piece *j* to piece *l*. Start at the tip and sew toward the outer edge. You do not need to offset the pieces; the seams between the aqua, pink, and yellow pieces should be aligned, as well as the tip and outer edge. Press.

14. Sew piece *k* to piece *m*, starting at the tip and sewing outward. Be sure to align the aqua pieces.

15. Align the tip of the piece *b* triangle with a hot pink strip to the tip of piece *j*. Mark down ¼″ from the tip. Start sewing at the mark, making sure to backstitch, and work outward. Press.

16. Add piece *k*, again aligning the tips, marking down ¼″ and sewing outward. Press.

17. Sew the seam between pieces *l* and *m*, aligning the tips, marking down ¼″ and sewing outward. Be sure to fold the other pieces out of the way. Press.

18. Sew the pentagon half to the hexagon half, making sure that the hot pink pieces, top and bottom, are aligned. Because the angles of the wedges on the left and right halves are different, you may need to open up the seam when you are pinning to ensure that when sewn the pieces will match up correctly.

Refer to pages 24–26 for information on sandwiching, quilting, and binding or go to tinyurl.com/quiltmaking-basics.

Quilting design

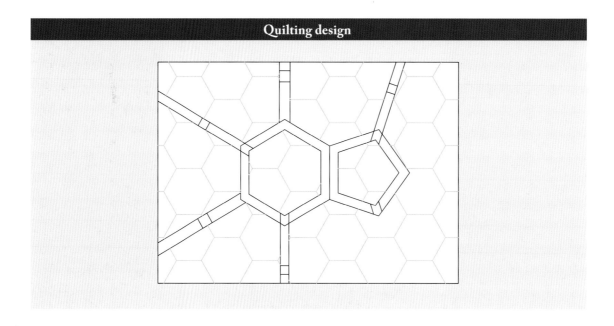

Circles

I was afraid of sewing circles for years. From pieced to appliqué, there are so many ways to add them to your quilts. The circles in this chapter use the freezer-paper method. I like this method because the circle is actually pieced into the block, as opposed to being appliquéd, and you don't have to work in quarters, as you would with a Drunkard's Path block. This method also allows you to piece arcs and irregular circles, like in *Cultured*.

Cultured is fun because we start small and you can be as wonky as you want with the small circles and then practice precision with concentric circles. *Echo* modifies the circle method to create arcs. *Aperture Science* combines circles with partial seams.

Drawing Large Circles

I always use a compass for smaller circles, but unfortunately a compass opens only so wide. To draw larger arcs and circles, I tie a string between a pushpin and a pencil. You want to be careful that as you are going around, the pencil maintains the same angle. Try to keep the string taut and the pencil upright. Use corrugated cardboard or a piece of cork to anchor the pin. **Figure A**

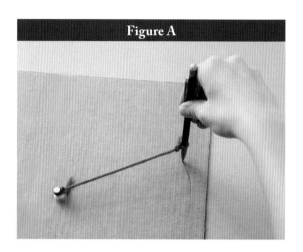
Figure A

Basic Technique

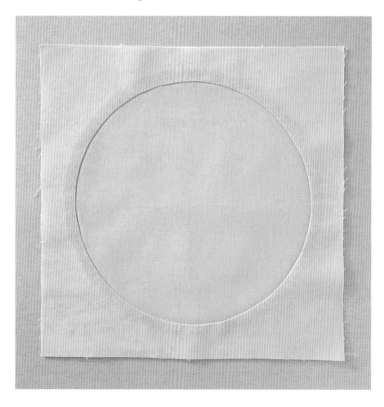

Materials

2 squares of freezer paper 2″ larger than the diameter of your circle

1 square of background fabric the size of the desired block

1 square of accent fabric the same size as the freezer paper

Gluestick

Make It!

1. Iron the 2 squares of freezer paper together (paper side to plastic side) on medium heat, no steam.

2. Mark the center of the freezer paper. Draw a circle on the paper side using the mark as the center. **Figure B**

Figure B

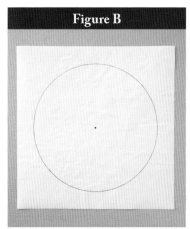

Figure C

3. Cut out the circle. You can discard the middle, but keep the outside intact.

4. Iron the freezer paper onto the wrong side of the background fabric, plastic side down. **Figure C**

Figure D

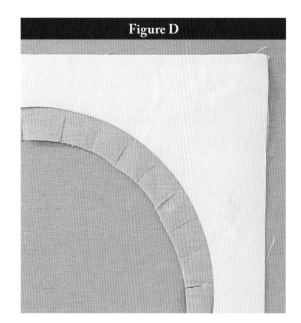

5. Cut out the center of the circle of the background fabric, leaving about ½˝ from the edge of the freezer paper. Snip the seam allowance around the circle every ½˝ to 1˝, stopping at least ⅛˝ away from the freezer paper. The larger the circle, the further apart the snips can be. **Figure D**

6. In 3˝ sections, glue at the edge of the freezer paper and smooth the fabric over the freezer paper. Continue all the way around the circle. Press using a dry iron on low heat.

 tip

A dab will do! You need only a very thin line of glue. It's best to glue about ½˝ from the edge of the freezer-paper circle, just close enough in to catch the clipped seam allowance. Using less glue will make it easier to remove the freezer paper later.

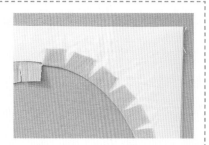

7. Place the accent fabric right side down on top. Again, in 3˝ sections, put glue on the clipped seam allowance that you just folded back. Try to keep the glue on the seam allowance and not on the freezer paper. Glue all the way around. Press. **Figure E**

8. When the glue is dry, carefully pull off the freezer paper. It's OK if it tears or leaves little bits behind; you will remove those at the end. Press.

9. Place the piece so that the accent fabric is on the bottom and the background fabric is on the top. Using a zipper foot, sew in the crease. You will slowly pull back the background fabric as you stitch in the crease. Backstitch at the beginning and end. **Figure F**

10. Trim the seam allowance to ¼˝. Press. **Figure G**

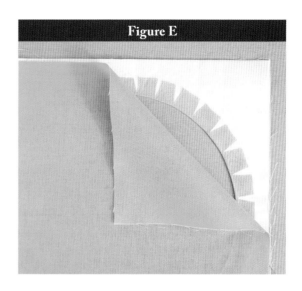

Figure E

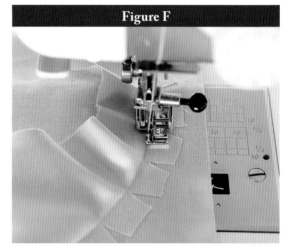

Figure F

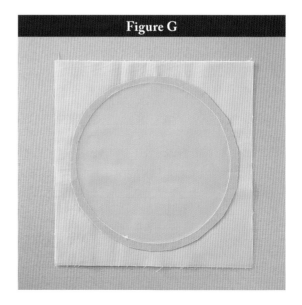

Figure G

Concentric Circles

This process is similar, but we will need additional tools to create perfect concentric circles. This is how the rim of the petri dish is created in *Cultured*. We'll create the inner circle first using the method on page 98; then we will create the outer circle.

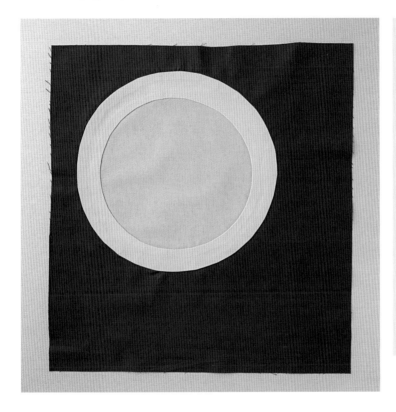

Materials

2 squares of freezer paper 2″ larger than the diameter of your outer circle

1 square of background fabric the size of the desired block

1 center circle already pieced (see directions on page 98)

Gluestick

Large piece of corrugated cardboard

Straight pin

Make It!

1. Create the inner circle using the Basic Technique (page 98). The background fabric will be the fabric for the outer circle.

2. Assemble the 2 layers of freezer paper. You may have to overlap the pieces by 1″ to create larger circles. Press the layers together, mark the center, and draw the circle on the paper side. *Do not* cut it out. Cut a small slit at the center of the circle.

3. Lay out the cardboard. Tape down the background fabric, wrong side up. Place the pin into the fabric and cardboard where you want the center of the circle to be. **Figure A**

4. Carefully place the freezer paper, plastic side down, onto the background fabric. The freezer paper should slide down over the pin through the slit in the middle. Iron around the drawn circle outward. It is not necessary to press the middle of the circle. **Figure B**

5. Starting in the center, carefully cut the freezer paper, lifting it away from the fabric. Cut out the inner circle and remove. *Be careful not to remove the pin.*

6. Cut out the center of the circle of the background fabric, leaving about ½˝ around the edge of the freezer paper. Snip around the circle every ½˝ to 1˝, stopping at least ⅛˝ away from the freezer paper. *Be careful not to remove the pin.*

7. In 3˝ sections, glue at the edge of the freezer paper and then smooth the fabric back. Continue all the way around the circle. Press.

8. Fold the center circle in quarters so that the center of the inner circle is at the point and the *right side* is facing out. Carefully place that point at the pin in the middle of the outer circle. Remove the pin and unfold the inner circle. Tape down the corners as you go so that you don't accidentally move the fabric. **Figure C**

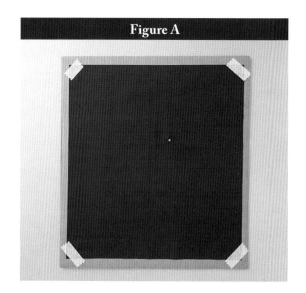

Figure A

tip I recommend corrugated cardboard because I always have boxes around to be recycled. You also could use foam core or thick cork, such as a trivet. If you have a hard floor, you can use a small piece of cardboard centered under the pin and tape the fabric directly to the floor. If you have carpet, I recommend finding a larger piece of cardboard, like an appliance box, and taping the fabric to the cardboard so that you have a hard surface to iron on.

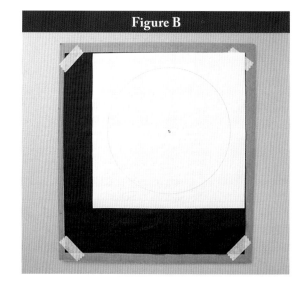

Figure B

9. Untape and fold back one corner at a time. Glue around the clipped seam allowance of the background fabric and then press the inner fabric back down. Continue around the entire circle. Press.

10. When the glue is dry, carefully untape all the layers of fabric and pull off the freezer paper. Press.

11. Place the piece so that the accent fabric is on the bottom and the background fabric is on the top. Using a zipper foot, sew in the crease. You will slowly pull back the background fabric as you stitch in the crease. Backstitch at the beginning and end.

12. Trim the seam allowance to ¼˝. Press.

Arcs

Arcs, which are used in *Echo*, are pieced almost exactly the same as the Basic Technique circles (page 98) except that you will be not be drawing a full circle on the freezer paper. You will still be using a double layer of freezer paper on the background fabric, but you will align the open bottom of the arc with the bottom of the background fabric. **Figure D**

Overlapping Circles

Making overlapping circles is really easy. Simply make one circle per the directions in Basic Technique (page 98). Use that piece as the background fabric and lay the freezer paper for the next circle over that one. The seams from the first circle will be a bit stiff when you turn them back, but that should be the only problem that you encounter. **Figure E**

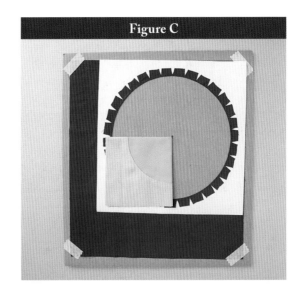

Figure C

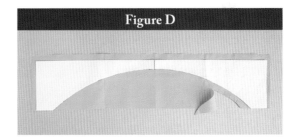

Figure D

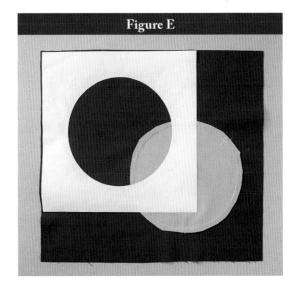

Figure E

Cultured

---------------- Finished quilt size: 38″ × 50″ ----------------

Inspiration

This was one of the first quilts I came up with for this book. My teacher-friend Amber was doing an experiment with her students to see what the dirtiest item was that they used daily. Spoiler alert: It was the cell phone! It was neat to see the petri dishes at the end and the different colors and shapes that the bacteria took.

Planning

I started with a circle for the petri dish and just drew circles until I came up with an arrangement that I liked. To define the edge of the dish I decided to add a dark gray border. This created the fun task of figuring out how to make concentric circles. I still wasn't satisfied until I shifted the petri dish off the quilt.

 tip If you are using graph paper, it's easy to break the circles in the petri dishes into blocks, shifting them slightly as needed. The graph paper also will help you determine the radii of the circles.

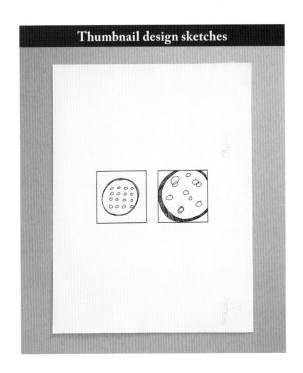

Thumbnail design sketches

Skills

If you haven't used the freezer-paper circle method (page 98) before, this is a great way to get in a lot of practice. What I want you to learn with this quilt is that you can use this method with any rounded shape; it doesn't have to be a perfect circle! You also get the chance to try overlapping circles by making the block with the bottom circle and then using the block again to add the top circle. Large circles work the same as the small ones, and concentric circles are possible with a few extra tools.

Study Hall Petri dishes are used to grow bacteria in a controlled environment. Petri dishes are filled with agar, a gelatinous substance that is used to support the growth of bacteria. Depending on the experiment, petri dishes are sealed and set aside for a set amount of time. The bacterial growth depends of the type of bacteria, how it was introduced to the agar, and the conditions of the experiment. Microbiologists use the results to create medicines and help doctors diagnose infections.

Materials

White: 1¾ yards

Blues and greens:
11 large scraps or fat quarters; distribute colors as desired

Dark gray: 1¼ yards

Green background and binding: 2¼ yards

Backing: 1¾ yards

Batting: 42″ × 54″

Other supplies:
Freezer paper
Compass
Cardboard
String
Gluestick

Cut It!

WOF = width of fabric

WHITE

- 1 strip 13″ × WOF:
  Subcut into 1 rectangle 13″ × 10″,
  1 rectangle 13″ × 6″,
  1 rectangle 13″ × 7½″, and
  1 rectangle 12″ × 6″.

- 1 strip 15″ × WOF:
  Subcut into 2 rectangles 14½″ × 8″,
  1 square 10″ × 10″,
  1 rectangle 10″ × 6″,
  1 rectangle 7½″ × 8″,
  1 rectangle 7½″ × 5½″, and
  1 rectangle 6″ × 4″.

- 1 strip 6½″ × WOF:
  Trim to 6½″ × 28″.

- 2 strips 3½″ × WOF:
  Trim to 3½″ × 38½″ and 3½″ × 28″.

- 1 strip 8″ × WOF:
  Trim to 8″ × 38½″.

BLUES AND GREENS

- 1 square 4″ × 4″
- 3 squares 5″ × 5″
- 5 squares 6″ × 6″
- 1 square 8″ × 8″
- 1 square 10″ × 10″

DARK GRAY

- 1 square 40″ × 40″

GREEN

- 1 rectangle 38½″ × 50½″
- 5 strips 2½″ × WOF for binding

FREEZER PAPER

- 2 squares 4″ × 4″
- 6 squares 5″ × 5″
- 10 squares 6″ × 6″
- 2 squares 8″ × 8″
- 2 squares 10″ × 10″
- 12 strips 40″ × width of paper

Make It!

Refer to Basic Technique (pages 98–100) for freezer-paper circles directions.

1. Iron the freezer-paper squares together in pairs.

2. Using a compass or freehand, draw circles on each of the smaller squares. There should be at least 1″ between the side of the circle and the edge of the paper. Cut out the circles.

3. To make a 40″ square, you will need to overlap 3 strips to create a 40″ width. Layer the other 3 pieces on top; then carefully press. *Do not use tape.* Repeat with the other 6 strips to make another double-layer 40″ square.

4. On one 40″ square draw a 36″-diameter circle. On the other draw a 38″ circle. Mark the centers. *Do not cut out the circles.*

Small Circles

5. Iron the small freezer-paper squares on the white background according to the diagram. You do not need to be exact.

6. Following the directions at the beginning of the chapter (page 98), piece all of the blue and green circles. **Figure A**

7. Join the blocks and add the borders according to the diagram. Fold the completed piece into quarters and mark the center. Unfold. **Figure B**

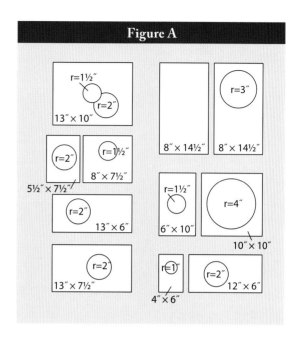

Figure A

Large Circles

8. Fold the dark gray square into quarters and mark the center on the wrong side. Unfold. Iron the 36″ freezer-paper circle to the back of the dark gray fabric, aligning the center marks.

9. Cut out the center of the freezer paper and sew the pieced center to the dark gray fabric according to the Basic Technique (page 98).

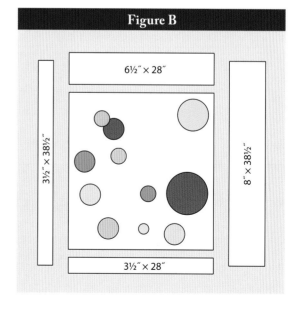

Figure B

10. Iron the 38″ freezer-paper circle to the wrong side of the green fabric. The freezer paper should overhang the top by 4½″ and the side by 5″. **Figure C**

11. Follow the steps for sewing Concentric Circles (page 101) to piece the center to the background.

12. Trim the edges even with the green background piece.

Refer to pages 24–26 for information on sandwiching, quilting, and binding or go to tinyurl.com/quiltmaking-basics.

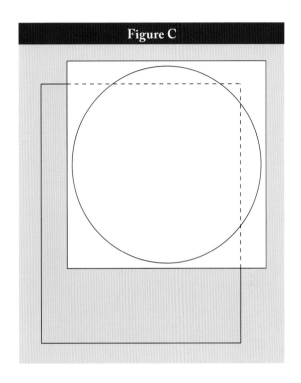

Figure C

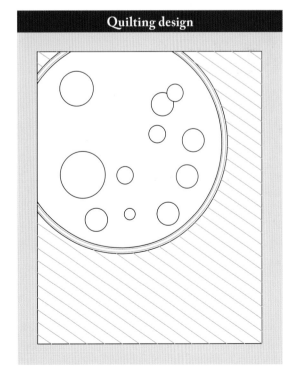

Quilting design

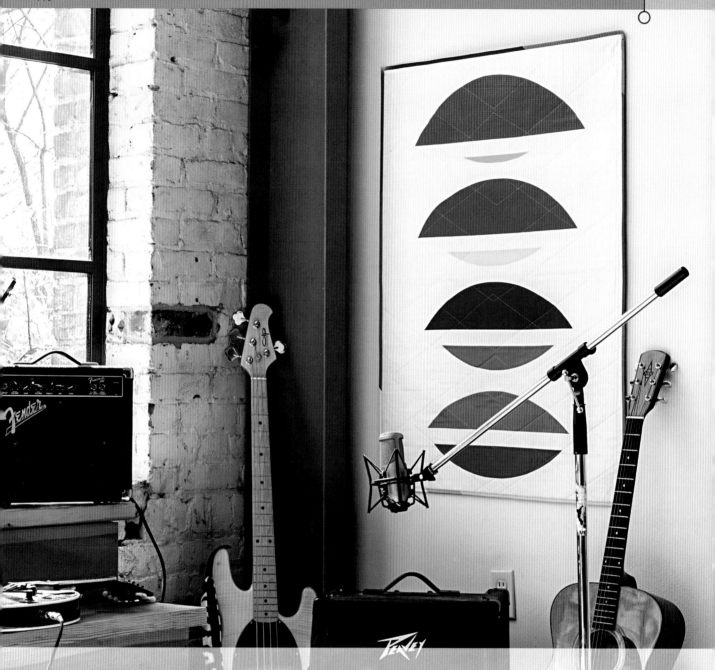

Echo

-- Finished quilt size: 29½˝ × 41½˝ --

Inspiration

As I was trying to come up with ideas for curves, sound waves kept coming to mind. I love the idea of what echoes do to sound waves and ran with it! For me this quilt is really about the colors. I saw a solids bundle and knew that the colors would be perfect! I've made this quilt on a larger scale and made the arcs patchwork to add some interest. Or you could make the background patchwork and make the arcs plain.

Planning

I tried a few different methods for the arcs. I tried making a circle and cutting off the sides to get four arcs, but the sizes weren't great and I could only use one fabric. Then I tried using a different radius for each arc, but they didn't look right. Ultimately I settled on using the same radius for each arc and making them progressively smaller. Then I got out my compass, drew a circle on graph paper, and made slices using the grid.

Skills

This quilt is really simple and should come together quickly after you get the hang of working with arcs instead of circles. This is also a great time to practice drawing large circles—although I've included patterns (page 115). If you decide to change the scale or draw your own pattern, remember that you just have to make one at the largest size and then trim it down or fold it down for the smaller sizes.

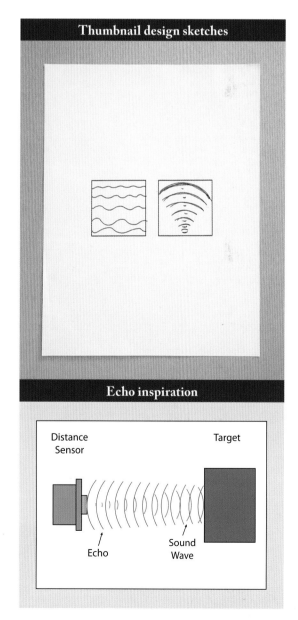

Thumbnail design sketches

Echo inspiration

Distance Sensor

Target

Echo

Sound Wave

Study Hall   An echo is a reflection of sound, caused by sound waves bouncing off an object. Because objects reflect sound differently, echoes can be used to find out properties—such as distance or terrain—of objects that can't be seen. Sonar is navigation using echoes and is employed by submarines, dolphins, and bats to name a few. They emit a sound and then listen to what is reflected back to them. By analyzing the differences in the sound, they are able to tell what is around them.

Materials

White: 2 yards

Pink: ¼ yard

Magenta: ¼ yard

Plum: ¼ yard

Lavender: ¼ yard

Purple: fat quarter

Periwinkle: fat quarter

Aqua: fat quarter

Teal: fat quarter

Backing: 1½ yards

Binding: ½ yard

Batting: 34˝ × 46˝

Other supplies:
Freezer paper
Pattern or string
Gluestick

Cut It!

WOF = width of fabric

WHITE
- 1 strip 8½″ × 30″ (*a*)
- 1 strip 6½″ × 30″ (*b*)
- 1 strip 5¾″ × 30″ (*c*)
- 1 strip 5″ × 30″ (*d*)
- 1 strip 5½″ × 30″ (*e*)
- 1 strip 3½″ × 30″ (*f*)
- 1 strip 2¾″ × 30″ (*g*)
- 5 strips 2″ × 30″ (*h* and *i*)

PINK (*a*)
- 7″ × 25″

MAGENTA (*b*)
- 6¼″ × 24″

PLUM (*c*)
- 5½″ × 22″

LAVENDER (*d*)
- 4¾″ × 21″

PURPLE (*e*)
- 4″ × 20″

PERIWINKLE (*f*)
- 3¼″ × 17″

AQUA (*g*)
- 2½″ × 15″

TEAL (*h*)
- 1¾″ × 11″

BINDING
- 5 strips 2½″ × WOF

FREEZER PAPER
- **a:** 2 strips 7″ × 25″
- **b:** 2 strips 6¼″ × 24″
- **c:** 2 strips 5½″ × 22″
- **d:** 2 strips 4¾″ × 21″
- **e:** 2 strips 4″ × 20″
- **f:** 2 strips 3¼″ × 17″
- **g:** 2 strips 2½″ × 15″
- **h:** 2 strips 1¾″ × 11″

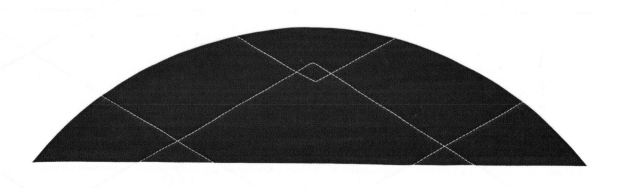

Make It!

1. Iron the 2 layers of freezer paper together for each size. Mark the center of the long edge. Trace the arcs onto the freezer paper or draw the arcs from a 13˝-radius circle. Cut out the arcs.

2. Fold each of the white strips used for arc blocks in half along the long edge and mark the centers. Unfold. Center the freezer paper on the wrong side of the fabric, aligning the bottom of the freezer paper with the bottom of the strip.

3. Piece the arcs to their corresponding white pieces according to the directions on page 103. **Figure A**

4. Sew the arc strips to the 4 remaining 2˝ white strips according to the diagram. **Figure A**

Refer to pages 24–26 for information on sandwiching, quilting, and binding or go to tinyurl.com/quiltmaking-basics.

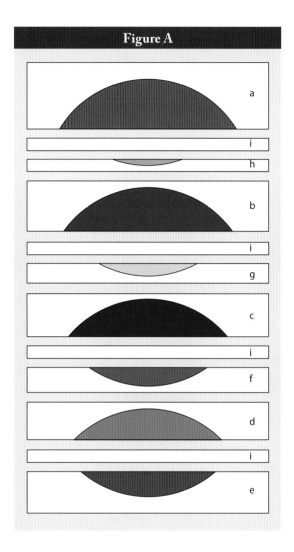

Figure A

Quilting design

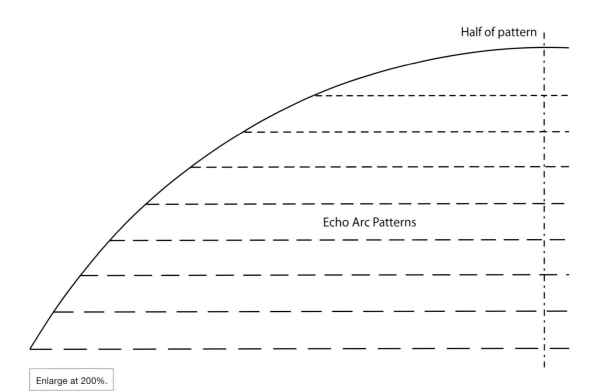

Half of pattern

Echo Arc Patterns

Enlarge at 200%.

Aperture Science

Finished quilt size: 52½″ × 52½″ • **Finished block size:** 17½″

Inspiration

This quilt came from playing *Portal*. In this computer game, the player tries to escape from a laboratory called Aperture Science, and the logo is like a camera shutter. I also love photography and have taken quite a few classes over the years, so I knew that there would be a way to blend these two.

Planning

I knew that I wanted to show different apertures and had originally planned this quilt to have the blocks in a column. It was fine, but it wasn't exciting. Finally I decided to try arranging the blocks in a grid with one different block. After playing with a few arrangements (and conferring with my husband), we decided on a camera block in the bottom right. You could move it elsewhere or omit it.

In photography a gray card is used to meter light. I used this concept to help me select the background color.

Skills

For each block you'll have to piece wedges to a hexagon using a partial seam at the beginning. This means that the seam does not lend itself to chain piecing because you don't start at the edge and have to backstitch when you start. This block centers the hexagon within a circle, but without using the concentric circle method. For the camera block you will have to sew concentric circles, but a bit wonky. There's a reason this project is at the end of the book!

Thumbnail design sketches

Study Hall   Aperture refers to how large the opening is and thus how focused the light is. Think about your eyes. When your pupils are dilated—like after an eye exam—they are large and let more light in, but less is in focus. In bright lights your pupils contract to let in less light. It's also easier to focus on more. Cameras work the same way. Overlapping blades open and close to change the size of the opening over the lens. This is the shutter. When it's dark you'll need a larger aperture to let in more light. This also means that less will be in focus. Photographers use larger apertures (such as *f*3.5) for portraits or details so that the background doesn't compete with the subject. In bright settings you can use a smaller aperture (say *f*14). Also, you use a smaller aperture when you want everything to be in focus, such as a landscape.

Materials

Light gray: 2½ yards

Medium gray: 1¾ yards

Black: 2 yards

White: 1 yard

Print: 1 square 7″ × 7″

Backing: 3½ yards

Binding: ¾ yard

Batting: 57″ × 57″

Other supplies:
Freezer paper
Patterns
Gluestick

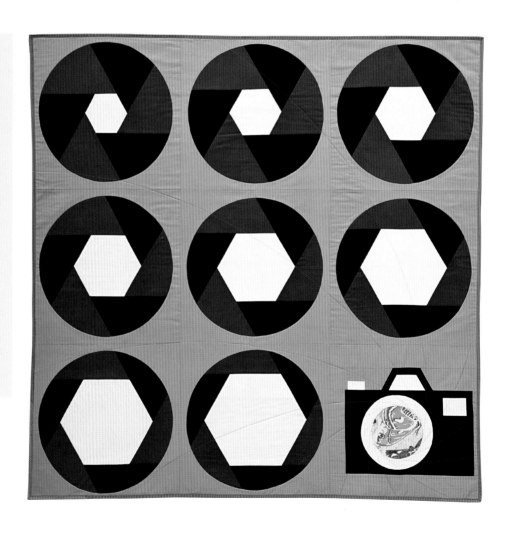

Cut It!

WOF = width of fabric

LIGHT GRAY

- 4 strips 18″ × WOF: Subcut into 8 squares 18″ × 18″, 2 rectangles 18″ × 3¼″ (*m*), 1 rectangle 2½″ × 3″ (*i*), 1 rectangle 2½″ × 2″ (*j*), 1 rectangle 15″ × 3″ (*k*), and 2 rectangles 10″ × 2″ (*l*).

MEDIUM GRAY (Figure A)

- 1 strip 13¾″ × WOF: Subcut into 8 of piece *x*.

- 1 strip 21¼″ × WOF: Subcut into 8 of piece *y*.

- 2 strips 9½″ × WOF: Subcut into 8 of piece *z*.

BLACK (Figure A)

- 1 strip 13¾″ × WOF: Subcut into 8 of piece *x*.

- 1 strip 21¼″ × WOF: Subcut into 8 of piece *y*.

- 2 strips 9½″ × WOF: Subcut into 8 of piece *z*.

- 1 strip 10″ × WOF: Subcut into 1 rectangle 10″ × 12″ (*a*), 1 rectangle 7¼″ × 4″ (*b*), 2 rectangles 1¼″ × 3¼″ (*c*), and 3 rectangles 1¼″ × 5″ (*d*).

WHITE

- 1 strip 11″ × WOF: Use to cut the 3 largest hexagons and the smallest hexagon.

- 1 strip 8½″ × WOF: Use to cut 1 each of the remaining 4 sizes of hexagons.

- 1 rectangle 2½″ × 1½″ (*e*).

- 1 rectangle 2½″ × 3¼″ (*f*).

- 1 rectangle 2¼″ × 5½″ (*g*).

- 1 square 9½″ × 9½″ (*h*).

BINDING

- 6 strips 2½″ × WOF.

FREEZER PAPER

- 6 squares 18″ × 18″.

- 2 squares 8″ × 8″.

- 2 squares 9½″ × 9½″.

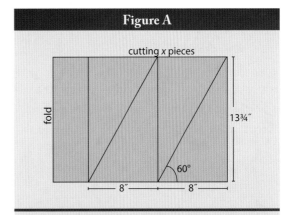

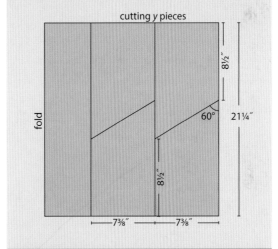

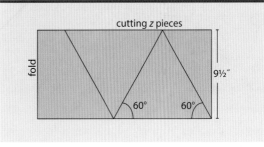

Figure A

Make It!

Shutter Blocks

1. Assemble the 18˝ square freezer paper into pairs. Draw a circle on each with an 8˝ radius and cut out.

2. Iron the freezer-paper pieces to the wrong sides of 3 light gray squares. Set aside.

3. Mark the centers of each hexagon by folding them into quarters.

4. Lay a black wedge x onto the smallest hexagon, aligning the raw edges and offsetting the point ¼˝. To sew a partial seam, start 1˝ from the edge of the hexagon with the gray overhanging piece, backstitch, and sew to the end of the side. Press. **Figure B**

5. Take a medium gray piece y and align it with the edge of the hexagon. Instead of overhanging like the first piece, the side will line up with the edge of the black piece that you just sewed. Sew all the way along the edge. Press. **Figure C**

6. Next sew a black piece z to the block like the last piece. Repeat with a medium gray x and a black y. **Figure D**

7. Flip back the tail of the first piece to expose the hexagon. Align the last medium gray z piece as you have the previous pieces and sew. Press. Flip the first piece so that it lies as flat as possible against the hexagon, similar to the original position when you sewed the first seam. The tail should now overlap the last medium gray piece. Sew along the edge until you reach where you started your first seam. Backstitch. Press. **Figure E**

8. Repeat Steps 4–7 with the remaining 7 hexagons.

9. Trim the blocks to 18˝ × 18˝, making sure to use the center of the hexagon as the center of your block.

10. Because your blocks have the hexagon centered and are the same size as your light gray background pieces, you can follow the Basic Technique (pages 98–100) to piece the center to the background. Reuse your freezer-paper pieces for the remaining blocks. **Figure F**

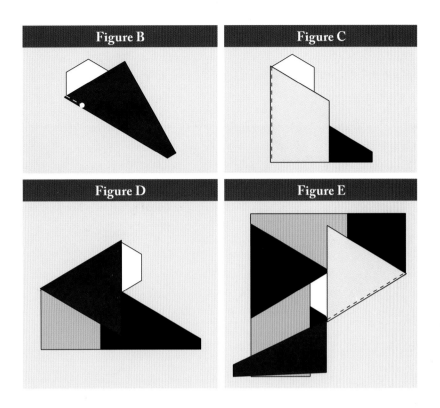

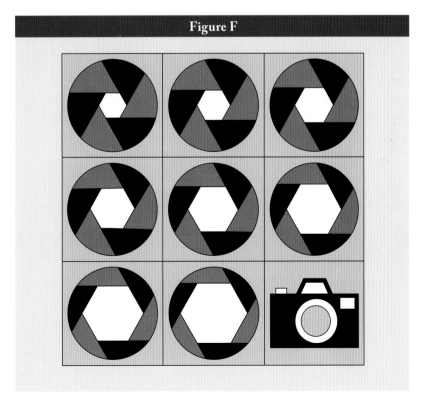

Camera Block

Refer to Figure G on page 123. Although the camera lens is made of concentric circles, I have opted to just eyeball it for a wonky look. If you would like the print to be centered, please follow the Concentric Circles instructions (page 101) instead of Steps 1 and 2.

1. Assemble the 8″ square freezer-paper pieces. Draw and cut out a 6″-diameter circle. Iron to the wrong side of the white 9½″ square *h*. Sew the print to the white using the Basic Technique for circles (page 98).

2. Assemble the 9½″ square freezer-paper pieces. Draw and cut out an 8½″-diameter circle. Iron to the wrong side of the black rectangle *a*. It should be approximately centered, but you do not need to be precise. Sew the white to the black using the Basic Technique freezer-paper method (page 98).

3. Sew a black rectangle *c* to white rectangle *f*. Press. Sew the other black rectangle *c* to the adjacent side. Press. Sew black rectangle *b* to the bottom.

4. Sew together the pieces from Steps 2 and 3, and then sew the light gray *l* rectangles to either side. Press. Sew a light gray rectangle *m* to the bottom. Press.

5. Sew 1 black rectangle *d* to the top of piece *g*. Trim at a 60° angle on both sides to create a trapezoid that is 5½″ at the base. Sew a black *d* piece to either side. Trim the black pieces to be even with the top and bottom of the trapezoid.

6. Cut light gray piece *k* at a 60° angle 3½″ from one end. Sew this piece to the left of piece *g*. On the remaining strip of *k*, measure over 6″ from the end and cut at a 60° angle. Sew to the left of piece *g*.

7. Sew white piece *e* to light gray piece *j*; then sew to light gray piece *i*. Sew this unit to the section from the previous step. Press; then sew the light gray rectangle *m* to the top and the camera body to the bottom. Press.

8. Trim to 18″ × 18″.

9. Assemble the blocks in rows, press the seams, and then sew the rows together. Press.

Refer to pages 24–26 for information on sandwiching, quilting, and binding or go to tinyurl.com/quiltmaking-basics.

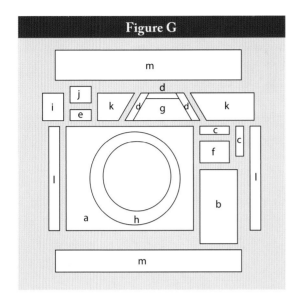

Figure G

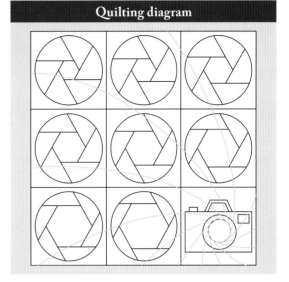

Quilting diagram

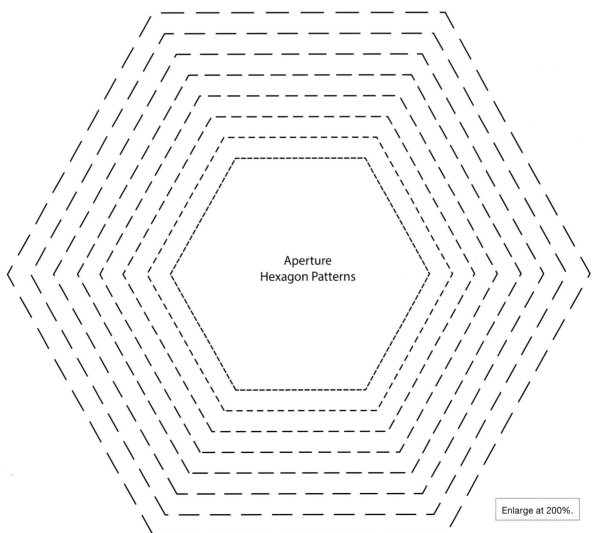

Aperture
Hexagon Patterns

Enlarge at 200%.

Appendix

Common Quilt Sizes

	Width (range)	Length (range)	Prepackaged batting
Miniature	Less than 36″	Less than 36″	
Baby/crib	36″–52″	36″–54″	45″ × 60″
Lap	40″–68″	50″–78″	
Toddler bed	40″–46″	65″–70″	
Twin	64″–72″	86″–96″	72″ × 90″
Full/double	70″–88″	88″–100″	81″ × 96″
Queen	88″–99″	94″–108″	90″ × 108″
King	94″–108″	94″–108″	120″ × 120″

Half-Square Triangles

I like to trim my HSTs when I'm finished so that they are more precise. With that in mind, all of the measurements given in the table below will produce blocks that are *slightly* larger than the finished measurement.

Finished HST	Square cut along 1 diagonal (yield: 2)	Square cut along 2 diagonals (yield: 4)
3″	4″	5¼″
3½″	4½″	6″
4″	5″	6¾″
4½″	5½″	7½″
5″	6″	8¼″
6″	6½″	9½″
7″	8″	11″
8″	9″	12½″
9″	10″	13¾″
Formula for custom-size HSTs		
No trimming	Finished size + ⅞″	$\sqrt{2a^2} = c + \frac{1}{2}''$
Trimming	Finished size + 1″	$\sqrt{2a^2} = c + 1''$

Note: Table measurements include seam allowances.

Slopes and Angles

Angle	Slope	Complementary angle	Slope	Where to use this
22.5°	5″/12″	67.5°	12″/5″	Hexadecagons; ¼ of a 90° angle (*Calculus*)
30°	4″/7″	60°	7″/4″	
45°	1″/1″	45°	1″/1″	Bias edges
54°	11″/8″	36°	8″/11″	Pentagon base angles (*Molecular*)
60°	7″/4″	30°	4″/7″	Equilateral triangles (*Molecular*)
63.33°	2″/1″	26.67°	1″/2″	Base angles of triangles inset in squares (*States of Matter*)
72°	40″*/13″	18°	13″/40″	Pentagon centers (*Molecular*)
90°				Squaring up blocks

Most cutting mats don't go up to 40″, and realistically that's a long way to measure. Alternatively you can use 20″/6.5″. The same goes for all of them: Since they are fractions, as long as you multiply or divide both the top and bottom by the same number, you can reduce or enlarge the ratio as much as you want.

Key Terms

Complementary angle: An angle that is very nice. Also, two angles whose sum is 90°. It's good to know these because when you cut fabric, the lines are used interchangeably, depending on the direction of your cutting mat.

HST: Half-square triangle.

Hypotenuse: The longest side of a right triangle, always opposite the 90° angle.

RST: Right sides together.

Slope: The slantedness of a line. A fraction gives this as rise (number of units up) over run (number of units over).

Ugly number: Not an integer. A number with a non–0.25, 0.5, or 0.75 decimal. These are hard for my students to deal with, and I don't care for them when I'm quilting. Lots of rounding takes place with ugly numbers.

WOF: Width of fabric.

About the Author

Alexandra Winston grew up in a sewing family. Both her mother and her grandmother were avid sewists and made outfits for her growing up. Since it was the 1980s, these involved quite a bit of neon and puffed sleeves, though not necessarily together. She became acquainted with Jo-Ann Fabric and Craft Stores at an early age and

Photo by Liz Yeakle

started sewing for herself in middle school. Her love of interior decorating led her to start sewing unique creations for her bedroom, like a black satin, velvet, and corduroy quilt.

Ali gave up sewing late in high school after a disheartening sewing disaster involving a Vera Wang dress pattern, boning, and lots of satin and lace. After college she worked as an architect, interior designer, furniture shop manager, and secretary (mostly at the same time!) before discovering that her passion was really in math education and sewing. Drawing on her art education at an engineering university, she loves to work art into her math classes and math into her sewing.

The teacher-quilter-author lives in Atlanta, Georgia, with her husband, Josh.